Les Diaboliques

D1713883

The French Film Guides
Series Editor: Ginette Vincendeau

From the pioneering days of the Lumière brothers' Cinématographe in 1895, France has been home to perhaps the most consistently vibrant film culture in the world, producing world-class directors and stars, and a stream of remarkable movies, from popular genre films to cult avant-garde works. Many of these have found a devoted audience outside France, and the arrival of DVD is now enabling a whole new generation to have access to contemporary titles as well as the great classics of the past.

The French Film Guides build on this welcome new access, offering authoritative and entertaining guides to some of the most significant titles, from the silent era to the early 21st century. Written by experts in French cinema, the books combine extensive research with the author's distinctive, sometimes provocative perspective on each film. The series will thus build up an essential collection on great French classics, enabling students, teachers and lovers of French cinema both to learn more about their favourite films and make new discoveries in one of the world's richest bodies of cinematic work.

Ginette Vincendeau

The first French Film Guides, publishing 2005, are:
Alphaville (Jean-Luc Godard, 1965) – Chris Darke
Les Diaboliques (Henri-Georges Clouzot, 1955) – Susan Hayward
La Haine (Mathieu Kassovitz, 1995) – Ginette Vincendeau
La Reine Margot (Patrice Chéreau, 1994) – Julianne Pidduck

Les Diaboliques

(Henri-Georges Clouzot, 1955)

Susan Hayward

UNIVERSITY OF ILLINOIS PRESS
URBANA AND CHICAGO

For the Clouzot Fans
Around the World

© 2005 by Susan Hayward
This edition produced by joint arrangement of I.B. Tauris & Co.
and the University of Illinois Press, and is available for sale only in North America.
1 2 3 4 5 C P 5 4 3 2 1

University of Illinois Press
1325 S. Oak St.
Champaign, IL 61820-6903
www.press.uillinois.edu

I.B. Tauris & Co., Ltd.
6 Salem Road
London W2 4BU
www.ibtauris.com

ISBN-10 (cloth): 0-252-03089-3
ISBN-13 (cloth): 978-0-252-03089-5

ISBN-10 (paper): 0-252-07330-4
ISBN-13 (paper): 978-0-252-07330-4

Library of Congress Cataloging-in-Publication Data

Hayward, Susan, 1945-
Les diaboliques / Susan Hayward.
p. cm. -- (French film guides series)
"This edition produced by joint arrangement of I.B. Tauris & Co.
and the University of Illinois Press"--T.p. verso.
Includes bibliographical references.
ISBN-13: 978-0-252-03089-5 (alk. paper)
ISBN-10: 0-252-03089-3 (alk. paper)
ISBN-13: 978-0-252-07330-4 (pbk. : alk. paper)
ISBN-10: 0-252-07330-4 (pbk. : alk. paper)
1. Diaboliques (Motion picture : 1955) I. Title. II. Series.
PN1997.D4585H39   2005
791.43'72--dc22   2005012918

Printed and bound in Great Britain by TJ Internationl Ltd, Padstow, Cornwall

Contents

Synopsis

Christina Delasalle (Vera Clouzot) is the wife of headmaster Michel Delasalle (Paul Meurisse), who runs a private boys' school in the outskirts of Paris. But Christina is tired of her husband's abusive behaviour towards her and his womanising. Michel's mistress, Nicole Horner (Simone Signoret), is equally fed up with his brutal behaviour towards her, and so the two women team up and decide to kill him by drowning him while making it appear as a suicide. When the body goes missing and sightings of the supposedly dead man are reported all over the city, the two women begin to panic. They must uncover what happened to the body, either before it is discovered or the interfering private detective (Inspector Fichet/Charles Vanel) unravels the women's plot. It transpires that the whole plot is a hoax invented by Michel and Nicole to put sufficient stress on Christina's heart and cause her to die of a heart attack. They succeed in causing her death (basically, by terrorising her). However, Inspector Fichet is on the ball and he catches them out, almost literally red-handed. Upon its release, the director Henri-Georges Clouzot urged all who saw the film not to reveal its surprise ending – one that still stands as one of the original 'shock' endings.

Introduction

Henri-Georges Clouzot (1907–1977): the man in focus

Henri-Georges Clouzot made only ten feature-length films.[1] Four of them won international prizes.[2] His first film, released in 1942, *L'Assassin habite au 21,* was a thriller – as was his last, *La Prisonnière* (1968). And the thriller is the genre we most readily associate with him. But not just any thriller. His take on the genre is dark, relentless, stifling, cruel. He strips away the mask of hypocrisy, shows life 'as it is', where people are weak and unable to change in a world that does not change. Clouzot's own life was dogged by illness and tragedy and it is only too easy to read the threatening nature of his thrillers through the optic of his personal life.[3] But, of course, that is only part of the story. What follows is an outline of this career.

Becoming a man of cinema 1907–1941

Henri-Georges Clouzot was born in the small provincial town of Niort (in south-western France) in 1907. By all accounts, his mother was a perfectionist and his father a failed businessman.[4] In 1922 his father was forced, through bankruptcy, to sell the family bookshop (in existence since 1836) and move his family to Brest. Clouzot's own life was also marked by this double edge of perfection and failure. Once in Brest he entered the Naval School, but was forced out because of his myopia. He then left for Paris to study diplomacy (by now he was 18 years old). Again he failed, this time because he did not come from money – as he puts it, he was 'quickly made aware that one doesn't belong'.[5] However, from these two early experiences he learned that he was drawn to the cinema and that he liked 'playing hide and seek with words, ideas and people'.[6] He then turned his hand, first, to theatre and, subsequently, to cinema as a playwright, lyricist and adaptor-screenwriter.[7] His success was modest. However, by the early 1930s he was working for Film Sonores Tobis (a Paris outlet of the German studios Universum Film AG), and in 1932 he was brought to Berlin to work on the French dialogue for the double-version films being made at Babelsberg Studios.[8] He lasted there for two years, after which he was sent home because, according to Clouzot, he got 'too friendly with one of his producers who was a Jew'.[9] The Berlin experience left its mark on Clouzot. He met Fritz Lang and F.W. Murnau. He developed a taste for German expressionist films, in particular the contrastive *chiaroscuro* lighting. Within a year of his return to Paris, however, he became seriously ill with pulmonary tuberculosis. This serious illness gave him 'a taste of death'[10] in his mouth – and he spent the next three years in various private sanatoriums, paid for thanks to friends who rallied round to support him. In 1938 he returned to Paris and befriended the actor Pierre Fresnay, who helped to get him back into the cinema business. In this same year he met the actor and singer Suzy Delair (who worked with Fresnay), with whom he had a 12-year relationship (she eventually left him after working with him on *Quai des Orfèvres*, 1947).

The auteur-metteur-en-scène has arrived 1941–1944

By 1940 France was an occupied nation; the Nazis controlled the northern half, and the southern half was governed by a German puppet regime (the Vichy government). Despite these difficult times, 1941 was the first major turning point for Clouzot. This was the year that the French film industry came under German control. Alfred Greven, the head of the German Continental Studios' branch in Paris (which now controlled all Paris-based studios), set up the Comité d'Organisation de l'Industrie Cinématographique (COIC) to manage the industry. Greven knew Clouzot from his Berlin days and asked him to direct the scriptwriting service at Continental. At first Clouzot declined, but then hunger and unemployment drove him to accept. His first adaptation, in his new capacity as director of screenwriting, was Georges Simenon's *Les Inconnus dans la maison* (Henri Decoin, 1942). Most significantly, he made the story blacker than the original – thus setting a trend for his own films to come, whereby he would considerably rewrite and make darker the original novel text. Interestingly, Stanislas-André Steeman – an author whom Clouzot used twice (*L'Assassin habite au 21* and *Quai des Orfèvres*) – felt that Clouzot was someone who would never be an adaptor and who could only 'build something after having *contemptuously* demolished any resemblance to the original, purely for the ambition of *effect*'.[11] This suggests not just a desire to impose an authorial stamp on the text but also an element of violence in Clouzot's working practice – one that Clouzot would see as closely identified with cinema. He once compared theatregoing with cinema in the following terms. 'On stage, it's like tennis, a very fast game which demands action from both sides' (the spectator and the actors), whereas cinema was the exact opposite: 'The spectator is placed in a situation where he might react at the beginning of the film but where his face is being punched repeatedly and as quickly as possible to annihilate him.'[12] A fairly brutal experience, then!

Clouzot was unimpressed by Decoin's film (based on his script) and so decided to turn his hand to directing himself. In this he was considerably enabled by the support of the popular screen couple Pierre Fresnay (his friend) and Suzy Delair (his lover), who agreed to be in his film. With *L'Assassin habite au 21* Clouzot undoubtedly cut his teeth as a filmmaker. He learned his craft the hard way. During the Occupation resources were extremely limited. As Suzy Delair explains, 'You only had two takes, so you had to be good.'[13] So Clouzot meticulously planned his film. He had a tight storyboard that had to be closely followed, and this allowed him, first, to work out how much studio space and what types of sets he would need and, second, to establish all the shots ahead of time. The result: the film was made in 16 days and cost virtually nothing. Clouzot's style, then, was a lean, sparse style. As the set designer Max Douy explains: '(He) made just what was needed, neither more nor less.'[14] Yet it was also always authentic. Clouzot could not abide anything that smelled of pretence.[15] And this leanness and authenticity also applied to his technique with his actors. He could not bear fabrication; the actor had to inhabit the moment. In order to get the effect he wanted (be it anger or tears) he would quarrel with actors, slap them – in short, shock them into the mood required.[16] Effectively, Clouzot wanted to strip his actors down to the bare bones of their acting, make them raw so that what they showed became more important than what they said. And he achieved this starkness (a cruel authenticity), first, by looking into each actor to discover what would serve his purpose, second, by exploiting their strengths and weaknesses and, third, by telling them what he wanted and making them rehearse until it was right. He was the boss, and he was tough and a perfectionist.

It was his second film, *Le Corbeau* (1943), which gained him the epithet of auteur-metteur-en-scène[17] but which also brought a heap of opprobrium onto his head. It was Cocteau who gave him this label, not only because he liked the film but because he perceived Clouzot's genius as both a master of *mise en scène* and the ubiquitous author of his film text. This notion of auteur-metteur-en-scène predates the 'auteur' debates of the 1950s, but it does point (unlike the single term 'auteur') to the extent of the labour involved in such an undertaking. Interestingly, the actor Louis Jouvet, who worked with Clouzot on *Quai des Orfèvres* and who also used this epithet, saw it as a more problematic dynamic than Cocteau. He saw a tension for Clouzot between the auteur and the metteur-en-scène; the dynamic of having to resolve technical issues and keep to his text made him over-preoccupied and in conflict with himself, in Jouvet's view.[18] Arguably, this tension is what gives an added edge of unease in Clouzot's films, making them more knife-edged than if he had been not been in conflict with himself.

Clouzot's film was inspired by Louis Chavance's 1937 script entitled *L'Oeil du serpent,* which was based on the Tulle affair (1922). Tulle is a small provincial town, and the affair involved a woman, Angèle Laval, who penned over 1,000 anonymous letters, signing them 'l'Oeil du Tigre'. Clouzot was fascinated by this story and wanted to make the film. Continental had reservations about it because, by 1943, letters of denunciation had become rife (after the war the number was estimated at some three million). This was precisely why Clouzot wanted to make the film; he was fed up with all the anonymous letters and wanted to denounce the practice.[19] The film was hit by controversy. Clouzot rowed with Greven and quit Continental two days before the première of his film. The film itself was so controversial and the publicity campaign so inflammatory that the German distributors ACE withdrew it from distribution in France. It was seen only in Switzerland and Belgium.[20]

From auteur maudit to auteur noir to auteur no more
1944–1968

In 1944, when France was liberated, numerous people (among them film industry personnel) were brought before the Comité d'épuration (the 'Cleansing Committee') accused of acts of collaboration with the enemy.

Clouzot was one of the accused, because he had worked for Continental (despite the fact that he had helped Jewish personnel and hid resistors).[21] He was banned from working in the industry for four years. His initial punishment was two years but a further two years were added. In the end he served just over three out of the four years. It is not difficult to see that he was punished as much for his working with Continental as he was for his film *Le Corbeau*.[22] The left perceived the film as a betrayal of the image of La France Résistante, the right saw it as anti-French propaganda. Interestingly Jean-Paul Sartre,[23] Simone de Beauvoir and Pierre Bost (all people of the left) sent a letter protesting against the sentence. To no avail.[24] Clouzot became an *auteur maudit*. It is worth making the point that Clouzot is rather difficult to pin down politically. He has been identified as a man of the right and yet he had as many associations with people of the left (for example, Simone Signoret, Yves Montand, Serge Reggiani, Sartre, de Beauvoir) as he had connections with the right (Pierre Fresnay being the most significant one). For this reason Clouzot remains ambiguous – which is why, of course, *Le Corbeau* met with such a double-edged response and contradictory reading.

Despite the ban, Clouzot continued to work in private on his next film project, *Quai des Orfèvres*. In this and his next film, *Manon* (1949),[25] Clouzot refined his system of working with actors. Louis Jouvet, who starred as the detective inspector in *Quai des Orfèvres*, provides interesting insights into Clouzot's craft as a director. 'What dominates with Clouzot is his lucidity. He explains the scene with amazing clarity. It is as if he were projecting the scene for you on the screen.' In short, Jouvet tells us, Clouzot's facility for taking away the 'technical jargon' made his actors feel secure.[26] This demystifying can be seen as part of Clouzot's economy of production practices. It saved on time and film. This does not mean that he was an easy director to work with, as we have seen. And we get a further sense of this when we recall how he left nothing to chance. Take, for example, his statement that 'to film an event there is only one placing of the camera. Once found, the rest follows.'[27] This apparent rigidity needs to be nuanced, however. While he would indeed shoot his chosen way, he was not impervious to listening to his actors if they thought there was another way to shoot the scene. According to Serge Reggiani (who worked with him on *Manon*), he would shoot both ways and choose the best shots. He could listen and negotiate – at least with the men, so Reggiani tells us. This was less the case for his female actors, with whom he was, to quote Reggiani, 'somewhat misogynistic'.[28]

A further way of understanding Clouzot's directorial style, which is particularly helpful when considering *Les Diaboliques*, is provided by Philippe Pilard's suggestion that he brought character and actor together and did not force the one into the other.[29] What Clouzot was not looking for, then, was a situation where the character inhabits the actor, but more one where actor, character, *mise en scène* and plot are in some kind of dramatic tension with the purpose, generally, of creating suspense – a practice not dissimilar, it could be argued, to the other master of suspense of this same period, Alfred Hitchcock. However, given that one of Clouzot's stars in *Les Diaboliques*, Simone Signoret, was well known for being an actor whose being was literally inhabited by the character, we can perhaps understand why there were difficulties for her in embodying a scheming murderer who was pretending not to be one! As Signoret herself explains, in order to make the plot of the film work she was supposed to act as if she were not the duplicitous schemer she was. However, she found it almost impossible, from the start, not to act her role as one who was guilty.[30]

Pilard also points out the other great strength of Clouzot's directorial style in that he made his characters real by bringing them into a situation which, at first, is fairly banal but which he pushes into the unbelievable.[31] A good example of this is the love triangle in *Les Diaboliques*, itself quite an ordinary, banal occurrence. However, as one of the schoolmasters rightly remarks, it is inconceivable that the two women (the wife Christina and the mistress Nicole) should be friends (which they are) when they should be rivals and enemies. But, of course, if the unbelievable were not made believable the plot simply would not work.

After the great success of *Quai des Orfèvres* (Cannes Best Director; a 5.5 million audience) and the slightly more modest, but still considerable one of *Manon* (Venice Golden Lion; 3.4 million spectators), Clouzot encountered the first of his real failures. He turned his hand to making a period comedy *Miquette et sa mère* (1950) – an adaptation of a stage play. An unusual departure, one might think, for someone so invested in portraying the dark side of life. But more unusual still when one considers that Clouzot thought that theatre was ill-suited to screen adaptation.[32] Nonetheless, it was during the shooting of this film that he met and fell in love with his future wife,

Vera Gibson Amado. They were soon married (1950), and then they took off to Brazil, Vera's native country. There, thanks to his wife's deeply superstitious nature and interest in the occult, he was introduced to voodoo practices. The Brazilian experience was to influence greatly Clouzot's take on his next project, *Le Salaire de la peur*, in which his wife had a role and which she helped to produce. Clouzot set up a production company named Vera Films and thereafter his wife was involved in his filmmaking practice until her untimely death (of a heart attack) in 1960. New precisions came into Clouzot's filmmaking craft as a result of *Salaire* – almost a final fine-tuning. Here he learned to accentuate contrasts and did so primarily on the level of narrative, editing (as a system of 'permanent shocks'),[33] image (in terms of volume and planes) and lighting (the '*chiaroscuro*' he had learned from Germany).

Although Clouzot still adhered to his strict production practices, it is from this film on that he began to experience difficulties in meeting his deadlines. Recurrent illness dogged him until the end of his career, but other factors affected his output as well. *Salaire* produced many delays. Clouzot had opted for the Camargue region to simulate Venezuela as a way of keeping costs low.[34] But bad weather, illness and accidents prevented the film from being shot within the designated nine weeks (September–October 1951). Things were brought to a halt by end-November and finishing the shoot had to be postponed by seven months. The original budget was doubled. Nonetheless, the film was acclaimed at Cannes in 1953, where it won the Grand Prix du Jury and earned international success (a 6.9 million audience in France).[35] In a similar vein *Les Diaboliques* also suffered considerable delays, albeit less than *Salaire*. Shooting took 16 rather than eight weeks to complete (see Chapter 1 for more details).

Clouzot was never again to attain the heights of these two great hits.[36] Although they are undoubtedly masterpieces of suspense and earned him the epithet of *auteur noir* he was never to know such acclaim again.[37] His failing was twofold. First, instead of capitalising on his successes by making a further thriller, Clouzot (strangely) made a film on his friend Pablo Picasso (*Le Mystère Picasso*, 1956). Second, he failed to realise that, by crafting his films in much the same way as before, he had misunderstood the changing climate of the times and the advent of a young people's cinema – soon to be known as *la nouvelle vague* – heralded in part by the work of young filmmakers such as Roger Vadim (*Et Dieu...créa la femme*, 1956, starring Brigitte

Bardot) and Louis Malle (*Les Amants*, 1958). Clouzot's next feature film did not come out until 1957 – *Les Espions*, a Cold War thriller – and it was, by Clouzot's standards, a failure (a 1.8 million audience). Critics saw it as both too confusing and old hat.[38] Indeed, in some ways the set and *mise en scène* are rather reminiscent of *Les Diaboliques*; it is a damp and dirty environment. Moreover, the spy narrative and characterisation seem to have more in common with *Alice in Wonderland* than with anything vaguely coherent. Critics were not much more persuaded by Clouzot's 1960 film *La Vérité* (co-scripted by his wife just before she died). In its classical narrative line (the love triangle) and traditional editing style it did not sit well when set against the vibrancy of the *nouvelle vague*. However, with its top-billed stars Brigitte Bardot and Sami Frey it nonetheless appealed to young audiences and it was a great commercial success (5.7 million spectators). Clouzot's next project was never completed due to a heart attack (*L'Enfer*, due out in 1964). And his last feature film, *La Prisonnière* (1968), was also something of a flop (a 1.3 million audience). Old-fashioned, stuck in his practices and uninventive and seemingly having lost his touch, the *nouvelle vague* consigned him thus to the purgatorial ranks of the *cinéma de papa,* and Clouzot was an auteur no more.

Conclusion

Yet Clouzot was an auteur, and, with the passage of time, he has become recognised as one.[39] He was the master of suspense through *mise en scène* and, as such, merits the frequent comparisons drawn between his work and Hitchcock's. Much like Hitchcock's work, Clouzot's films were 'not a question of realism, nor of truth, but a sort of reality created within and by the film itself'.[40] As with Hitchcock, the focus on detail is there, always, whether it be in the soundtrack, the décor or the costumes. Although he once stated that he 'lacked something Hitchcock and Billy Wilder have, a sense of humour', he certainly was not intending to make a modest remark.[41] Hitchcock's humour is lighter, more playful. Clouzot's is dark, slightly nasty. Furthermore, in terms of difference, Clouzot's working with *mise en scène* is bleaker, more oppressively detailed and, therefore, darker in its horror than Hitchcock's. It is also more decrepit – not for him the glamorised settings or characters we often find in Hitchcock's work. Many of Clouzot's characters, like the settings, are redolent with decay – certainly deprived of glamour. Where the two filmmakers do rejoin, however, as Clouzot readily acknowledges, is in their preoccupation with 'certain violent elements'.[42] The cruelty of *Les Diaboliques* resonates well with that of *Vertigo* (1958) and *The Birds* (1963), and the mounting terror in Clouzot's film easily anticipates *Psycho* (1960).

Furthermore, in terms of his auteur status, it is worth looking at his overall filmmaking practice. Generally speaking, Clouzot had total control of his film from script through storyboard to shooting script, and from script to final product. In most cases, he radically altered the original and adapted the text to make it his own. He mixed studio practice with location shooting and did so effectively at a time when location shooting was not common. Paradoxically, although rigid and meticulous in his preparations, he was able to be flexible once shooting and then editing took place.[43] He worked with a fairly constant team of technicians and actors, beginning, most importantly, with the camera operator Armand Thirard, who taught him his craft.[44] Thirard was Clouzot's director of photography on seven out of his ten feature films.[45] William-Robert Sivel was his sound operator in all but one film. Clouzot's scriptwriter brother Jean (under the pseudonym of Jérôme Géronimi) assisted him on four of his films. Most of the art directors Clouzot worked with came from the pre-war poetic realist tradition. Both Andrei Andrejew and Max Douy, respectively, were associated with three of his films. Georges Wakhévitch designed *Miquette et sa mère*. Léon Barsacq was responsible for the sets of *Les Diaboliques*. In terms of actors, he regularly used Pierre Larquey and Noël Roquevert in secondary roles. Pierre Fresnay, Suzy Delair and Louis Jouvet were recurring star personas in his films until quarrels (Fresnay and Delair) or death (Jouvet) made them no longer accessible. His wife, Vera, starred in three of his films. Although she was not a trained actor she was determined to star in his films, and, thanks to their continuing appeal, she is still – along with the stars listed above, as well as Paul Meurisse, Yves Montand and Simone Signoret – a known name (albeit an actor of limited talent).

With Clouzot we are confronted with the master of making the banal unbelievable – and he achieves this, as we noted, by pushing a trivial situation to its limits. Not satisfied with this act of transformation alone, Clouzot takes us one step further and proceeds to make the unbelievable the central focus of his films while at the same time getting us to suspend disbelief. In other words, the narrative and events therein, although fundamentally and rationally unbelievable, are systematically naturalised and pass as normal. A brilliant masquerade! And it is in this sleight of hand that he thrills us all, and chills us to the bone. As the trailer advertising the release of *Les Diaboliques* immodestly makes clear, with each film his ability to frighten us gets better: 'More mysterious than *Le Corbeau*! More fascinating than *Quai des Orfèvres*! More spellbinding than *Manon*! More terrifying than *Le Salaire de la peur*! ... *Les Diaboliques*!'[46]

Notes

1   In the 1960s he also made a series of musical documentaries for television, filming the orchestral concerts of conductor Herbert von Karajan.

2   Cannes Best Director for *Quai des Orfèvres* (1947); Venice Golden Lion and Méliès for *Manon* (1949); Cannes Grand Prix for *Le Salaire de la peur* (1953) – Charles Vanel won Best Male Actor; Delluc for *Les Diaboliques* (1955).

3   As Stanley Goulder in his review of *Les Diaboliques* makes clear: '[F]or Clouzot, as for Buñuel, death is never serene...'; 'The necrophilist', in *Films and Filming* 1 (10), 1955, p. 8.

4   Bocquet, Jose-Louis (1993), p. 8.

5   Henri-Georges Clouzot, quoted in Bocquet, (1993), p. 9.

6   Clouzot, quoted in Bocquet (1993), p. 9.

7   In 1934 he wrote a song for Marianne Oswald (a refugee from Moselle), *Jeu de massacre*, which was a great hit (Bocquet (1993), p. 16). The tone of violence in Clouzot's lyrics should not escape our notice, however.

8   At that time, with the advent of sound, studios needed to produce multiple language versions of their films for export. UFA was no exception, and was one of the strongest competitors to the American studios (for example, Paramount had Paris-based studios producing multi-lingual versions of their films).

9   Clouzot, quoted in Bocquet (1993), p. 16.

10   Clouzot, quoted in Bocquet (1993), p. 17.

11   Stanislas-André Steeman, quoted in Bocquet (1993), p. 44; my emphasis.

12   Clouzot, quoted in Bocquet (1993), p. 59.

13   Suzy Delair, quoted in Bocquet (1993), p. 28.

14   Max Douy, quoted in Bocquet (1993), p. 46.

15   For example, even though his film *Le Salaire de la peur* was shot in the Camargue because there was not enough money to go to Venezuela, Clouzot insisted that sets and props be as authentic as possible – to the extent that Charles Vanel had to be immersed in real crude oil when he was rescued by Yves Montand. Clouzot refused to go for the soft option of coloured water.

16   His 'brutality' knew no bounds, it would appear. He regularly slapped not only women actors – as Suzy Delair can testify (Bocquet (1993), p. 29) – but also

men (Bertrand Blier in *Quai des Orfèvres*, for example (ibid., p. 47). To get the effect he wanted from Brigitte Bardot for the murder scene in *La Vérité* (1960), he got her drunk and then proceeded to slap her until she cried hysterically (see notes in *Edinburgh Film Festival Catalogue* 57, 2003, p. 126).

17 Phillipe Pilard (1969), p. 18.

18 Louis Jouvet quoted in Bocquet (1993), p. 48.

19 Ibid. pp. 33–34.

20 For more details of the controversy on *Le Corbeau*, see Bocquet (1993), pp. 33–38, and for the press reviews collated at the end of the publication of the *Le Corbeau* script, see *Avant-scène du cinéma* 186, 1977.

21 For more details, see Bocquet (1993), p. 38.

22 Clouzot made only two films with Continental. Compare that figure with the number of films made with Continental by some of his French contemporaries: Decoin made three, Tourneur four, Cayatte four and Pottier five. All but Cayatte (who was not sanctioned) got a seven-or eight-month ban (Bertin-Maghit, Jean-Pierre (1989), p. 406 passim.).

23 In 1943 Clouzot worked for three months with Sartre on a script for a film *Chambre obscure*, which never came to anything. Neither of them was satisfied with it. But it sealed a friendship.

24 Bocquet (1993), p. 38.

25 This strange updating of the narrative into the near-contemporary has Manon being transported on a boat taking Jews in secret to Palestine (rather than Louisiana, as in the novel). There she meets her death, as do the Jews, who are massacred by the Arabs. Needless to say, the reaction to this film from the left was one of considerable outrage and Clouzot was accused of anti-semitism (for details of reviews of this film, see *Avant-scène du cinéma* 463, 1997, p. 6). But it is worth making the point that, just because he was a man of the right, this did not mean that he did not hold liberal beliefs. In *Quai des Orfèvres* he paints an amazing portrait (for its time) of Jouvet as the father of a mixed-race son upon whom he dotes. He had wanted to make a film on the Algerian situation, giving all sides of the question, but the proposal was effectively sidelined by producers when they asked for too many changes to the original idea (see Clouzot, quoted in *Avant-scène du cinéma* 463, 1997, pp. 105–106). He had also wanted to make a film on Indochina but was blocked (Bocquet [1993], p. 87). Nor did he behave dishonourably during the Occupation.

26 Jouvet, quoted in Bocquet (1993), p. 46.

27 Clouzot, quoted in Pilard (1969), p. 27.

28 Serge Reggiani, quoted in Bocquet (1993), p. 52.

29 Pilard (1969), pp. 41–42.

30 Simone Signoret (1978), p. 129.

31 Pilard (1969), p. 42.

32 Bocquet (1993), p. 59.

33 Clouzot, quoted in Bocquet (1993), p. 84.

34 To be completely precise, because Latin America was off-limits financially, Clouzot had suggested Spain. But Yves Montand, one of his stars, refused on the basis that he could not work in a country under Franco's dictatorship. So the Camargue was the compromise.

35 For more details, see Yves Montand's recollection, in Hamon, Hervé and Rotman, Patrick (1990), pp. 176–183.

36 *Le Salaire de la peur* obtained an audience of 6.9 million and *Les Diaboliques* netted 3.7 million spectators.

37 The term *'auteur noir'*, ascribed to Clouzot, is quoted by Pilard (1969), p. 18 and Bocquet (1993), p. 51.

38 The critic Henri Jeanson even went so far as to say that Clouzot 'had done a Kafka in his pants' (quoted in *Avant-scène du cinéma* 463, 1997, p. 10).

39 Clouzot's achieving auteur status was internationally consecrated by the 2003 Edinburgh Festival (see notes in *Edinburgh Film Festival Catalogue*, 57, 2003, pp. 114–127).

40 Clouzot, quoted in Pilard (1969), p. 42.

41 Clouzot, quoted in Pilard (1969), p. 42.

42 Clouzot, quoted in Kemp, Philip 'Hitching posts', *Metro Magazine* 105, 1996, p. 34.

43 He is quoted as saying: 'No matter how much I prepare in advance, I am always modifying on the set, to say nothing of when editing'; Pilard (1969), pp. 50–51.

44 Bocquet (1993), p. 28.

45 A little note of irony: Thirard was Vadim's director of photography for *Et Dieu … créa la femme*. Clearly, he was capable of being modern even though his great partner Clouzot apparently was not.

46 Details of these trailers can be found on the DVD of *Les Diaboliques* ('C'est la vie' TF1, copyright 2002).

1 Production contexts

Obtaining the rights and adapting the novel

Clouzot's adaptation of Pierre Boileau and Thomas Narcejac's *Celle qui n'était plus* (*She who was no more*, 1952), *Les Diaboliques*, was one of his greatest commercial successes. Some say it was his masterpiece – certainly, it is one of the most terrifying films ever made.[1] Clouzot was always on the outlook for novels to adapt. An inveterate insomniac, he had plenty of time to devour books by the dozen, even though he passed the job of the initial selection onto his wife Vera.[2] It was she who, having once read Boileau and Narcejac's novel, persuaded him to obtain the rights.[3] He did so and blocked those rights for a year, thus effectively preventing Alfred Hitchcock from getting his hands on the story. This novel was the first in a string of successful collaborative works by Boileau and Narcejac – and Hitchcock did not have to wait long before their third novel, *D'Entre les morts* (*From the Dead*) was made available to him and became his own masterpiece, *Vertigo* (1958). Undoubtedly Hitchcock's adaptation bears a stronger resemblance to the original story than does Clouzot's. But, as we know, Clouzot only used the original as a starting point, as an idea for where he wanted to go. In this case it was 'the idea of a hoax' that attracted him.[4] In the original story, just as in Clouzot's version, we are bamboozled until the end.

The title of the film took some time to refine. Originally it was to be called *Les Veuves/The Widows*. Eleven weeks into shooting the title was changed to *Les Démoniaques*. Neither title seemed viable. Eventually Clouzot came up with *Les Diaboliques*. But, because this title already referred to a collection of short stories by the 19th-century author Barbey d'Aurevilly, Clouzot was given permission to use the title only on the condition that he paid homage to its originator. This he does by quoting d'Aurevilly in the opening credit sequence.[5] D'Aurevilly's text, which consists of a series of rather scabrous stories about women, rather outstrips in nastiness and vulgarity Clouzot's own film. The stories are quite close to pornography (at least, for the time), and are as much about the desire of men to vanquish women as they are about the diabolical nature of women, who will stop at nothing to ensnare and victimise their man.[6]

Clouzot did not find the adaptation of Boileau and Narcejeac's novel at all easy, primarily because he wanted to give his wife a really good role to make up for her small part in *Le Salaire de la peur*. But the original did not lend itself to a great role for her since the primary female figure was a doctor with decidedly 'masculine' ways, who, as it transpires by the end of the novel, is a lesbian. In other words, that particular role, of a tough, conniving mistress, was far too estranged from Vera Clouzot's physically fragile and distinctly feminine person. The only other female character in the novel was the supposed victim, Mireille, and she hardly had a role at all. Clouzot struggled for 18 months until he and his co-scriptwriter brother (Jean, aka Jérôme Géronimi) came up with the idea of locating the story in a boys' boarding school.[7] This freed his thinking and allowed him to reconstruct the triangular relationship in a completely different manner. In the novel, it is the two women – Lucienne the doctor, and Mireille the wife – who are in reality plotting to do away with the husband, Ravinel. Unbeknown to Ravinel (who is working under the assumption that Lucienne is only his mistress), it is in fact the two women who are lovers. Their scheme is to terrorise him into having a heart attack so they can get their hands on his life insurance policy and run away to the sunny south of France. The hoax (in relation to the reader) is that Ravinel and Lucienne appear to be plotting to kill Mireille. However, at the end of the novel it transpires that Mireille's death has been faked. So the mysterious notes left around the house for her husband to discover and the odd noises are not Mireille's ghost, as Ravinel believes (as he goes increasingly insane and becomes physically weaker), but in fact the real Mireille. In the end, unable to stand the guilt any longer, he commits suicide. Thankfully for the women, this eventuality (suicide) will not prevent them from getting the money because it is covered by a two-year exclusion clause (after the first two years the policy will cover the person's death, no matter what the cause).

Clouzot decided to reverse the tale, and in his script (as already mentioned) it is the husband and his mistress who plot against the wife (who is now the one with the weak heart). But we do not realise this until the very end of the film, when they successfully bring about her collapse and death by terrorising her. We have a similar triangle to the novel, but a different set of dynamics. The wife, Christina (Vera Clouzot), is married to the ruthless and sadistic headmaster Michel (Paul Meurisse), with whom she runs a private boarding school just outside Paris. Nicole (Simone Signoret), the mistress, is a science teacher. To all appearances Nicole and Christina have ganged up against Michel because he behaves so brutally towards them both. They enter into a complicit relationship against him and ostensibly seem to be plotting to do away with him. They drug him, drown him in a bathtub, throw him into a swimming pool and leave him for dead. But, like a ghost, he returns to haunt Christina and, eventually, she succumbs to a heart attack.

In order to give his wife a big enough part, Clouzot completely inverted the sexual dynamics and heterosexualised the original text. It is not necessarily the case, however, that Clouzot 'erased' the lesbian element because of the especially homophobic nature of the period, or because of concerns about censorship. He had, after all, introduced a lesbian character into his film *Quai des Orfèvres* (who did not exist in the original novel). So he was not afraid, as Judith Mayne points out, to deal with questions of sexuality and gender.[8] And, as we shall see, Clouzot was unable to (or chose not to?) delete completely the lesbian thread of the original text. For now, suffice it to say that the effect of 'straightening' the text meant that Vera Clouzot now occupied Ravinel's original place and Paul Meurisse took on Mireille's. Small wonder Boileau and Narcejac were somewhat put out. In Narcejac's view, Clouzot had made the story brutal, a mass that 'knocks you out' – suggesting, through his choice of words, that the delicateness of the queer in the novel has been erased and replaced by the thuggery of the heterosexual in the film. He was also of the opinion that, whereas *Celle qui n'était plus* was like euthanasia, in *Les Diaboliques* it was out and out murder.[9] The tone is certainly more violent in the film than in the novel, reminding us of Clouzot's words about the cinematic experience and its resemblance, to his mind, to a boxing match.[10]

Casting

Having already decided to cast Vera in the role of Christina, Clouzot needed
to make sure he had the right kind of support to help carry her through such
a developed role. He turned to Simone Signoret, who, along with her husband
Yves Montand, he had somehow managed to befriend. Their friendship was
by all accounts a tumultuous one – unsurprisingly, since they came from
opposite sides of the political spectrum – but one which was forged during
holidays spent in Saint-Paul de Vence (in the south of France) and, more
particularly still, during the time Montand was shooting *Le Salaire de la
peur*.[11] Signoret was under no illusion as to why she had been offered the part;
Clouzot did not especially rate her talents, even though she was by this time
an internationally recognised star. He thought that *Casque d'or* (undoubtedly
her best performance to date) was a 'non-film'.[12] However, he also knew that
Vera was not an actor, and so he wanted someone who was a friend to work
with her.[13] Signoret is very clear in her autobiography that it was Vera
who wanted the big role, in the meantime pretending that her husband was
forcing her into it. Nor was she easy to work with. Signoret's description of
her is generous but makes it clear that she was a woman of extremes.[14] So,
between Clouzot's caustic nature and his wife's difficult ways, she was caught
between a rock and a hard place. Small wonder that relations soured and that,
towards the end of the shooting, the three of them were no longer speaking
to each other[15] – a situation not improved upon by the fact that Signoret had
agreed to an eight-week contract, but in the end shooting took 16 weeks.
Clouzot had covered himself well and Signoret had failed to read the small
print, so she was obliged to stay on. Moreover, when it came to pay day, she
was paid only for the eight weeks she had signed up to.[16] As she rightly
points out, it was a mistake to work *en famille*. Everyone knew each other's
(private) faults and this knowledge clouded judgments in the professional
arena of the studio.[17] Yet the frictions and silences worked to the film's
advantage: Signoret's annoyance gets internalised, as an inner violence
waiting to let loose that is dramatically terrifying. Vera Clouzot's distance
from her former friend in real life plays admirably to her advantage in
the later stages of the film, when she becomes more forceful as a character
and starts bossing Nicole/Signoret about – indeed, the force of her dislike
rings true.

Clouzot used Signoret in a twofold way, then: first, her star cachet to bring in audiences (much as he had used Montand's singer-star image for *Le Salaire de la peur*); second, her willingness to help friends (she had previously appeared in a film, *Sans laisser d'adresse* (Jean-Paul Le Chanois, 1951), to give moral support to Danièle Delorme). Paul Meurisse is far less gracious than Signoret about the way she was exploited:

> Well, with his wife Vera, who if she was an actor then I am a Chinaman, he must have been wallowing in happiness! But at what a price! How many hours were spent finding clever ways of lighting her face to give it even a suggestion of expressiveness! How much teeth-grinding and muffled dissent on Simone Signoret's part, who was watching her talent being used to support the total emptiness of her co-star. But even more craftily, they muted the light on her so that her beauty would not squash still further the insignificance of Vera's face.[18]

Harsh words, but disinterested ones, and, if we look closely at the lighting, undoubtedly Signoret is held more in half-tones than Vera Clouzot.

This same tendency of trying to sacrifice Signoret for the sake of his wife comes through in the actual shooting. Vera Clouzot has 121 solo shots as opposed to Signoret's 72. Half of Clouzot's shots of Vera are in close-up or medium close-up (9 CUs and 51 MCUs), three times the number of those reserved for Signoret, who has only 18 (3 CUs and 15 MCUs). We could be excused for thinking that Vera Clouzot is the only star of this film, not the top-billed star Simone Signoret (and, of course, as we know, it was the Clouzots' wish that she, Vera, should stand out). However, even though she has only half the presence in terms of solo shots as Vera Clouzot, Signoret, through her sheer actorly presence, dominates the film.

Meurisse was cast as Michel, and seemed a natural for it, associated as he had become with roles of the icy but distinguished villain, several of which he had played opposite Signoret: *Macadam* (Blistène, 1946), *Impasse des deux anges* (Tourneur, 1948). Clouzot had known Meurisse since his early days, back in 1939, when he was starting out his career as a singer-actor (helped along by Edith Piaf, his then lover). He gave up singing and turned to the theatre, which subsequently became his first, very successful, artistic medium. But he also regularly crossed over and made films. Meurisse's very distinct film acting style came about as a need to demarcate himself from the two big leads of the 1940s: Pierre Fresnay and Louis Jouvet. Meurisse managed to distinguish himself from the sophisticated urbanity and elegance of Fresnay and Jouvet's dry humour by choosing film roles that required an inscrutable cold indifference tinged with biting sarcasm or caustic wit. His role as Michel for *Les Diaboliques* suited him, therefore, to a tee.

With regard to Clouzot's legendary tyrannical treatment of actors, Meurisse does not disabuse us on the filmmaker's need to dominate women, nor on the fact that he and Clouzot had some cross moments.[19] He does, however, dispel one myth that has held currency about this film – namely the famous bathtub scene. Rumour had it that, in order to give an authentic feel to the shot, Clouzot immersed Meurisse in cold water. Nothing could be further from the truth, Meurisse tells us. It took two days to shoot this scene and Clouzot had contracted Meurisse for only 13 days, so he certainly could not afford to have his male star laid up with pneumonia. Instead, the sequence was shot with Meurisse immersed in hot water and, in between takes, he was bundled into a heated cabin, dried off, dressed in dry clothes and given whiskey hot toddies. In effect, he remained pleasantly drunk during those two days.[20]

When we recall that Clouzot once said of actors: 'I can make any beginner act. But what I detest are actors who think'.[21] We can begin to see what Signoret was up against – and, indeed, to a lesser degree, Meurisse (because he was around for only two weeks of the shooting). Both these actors exude intelligence – Meurisse a cold calculating one, Signoret one of strength and brilliance. And, in fact, in this film she has to demonstrate cynical intelligence – the plot largely depends on her ability to dupe us, the audience, and for that to happen she has to dupe Christina (a very complex double-play). So Clouzot, in the end, was reliant on the very thing he claimed to detest! In relation to stars, Clouzot also said that he had to 'tame' their star persona and make their myth work for him.[22] In his efforts to make Signoret more tractable he de-sensualised her (partly through the choice of functional clothing for her to wear), and focused on her hard side. He brought out more the scheming bitch Dora of *Les Manèges* (Allégret, 1950) than the sensuous Marie of *Casque d'or*, he also endeavoured to make her less ambiguous. Even the haircut – the short-cropped hair – was a way to destabilise her sensuality and erotic power. However, to a degree this backfired, first because the blondness is glamorous and, second, because Signoret liked the new look.[23] Despite Clouzot's attempts to neutralise her, neither Signoret's natural authority nor her ironic insolence disappears in this film. In a way, these traits are greatly assisted by casting her as a crisp and no-nonsense science teacher.

Clouzot claimed to like to 'fascinate' his actors, to 'read' into them.[24] This suggests a double form of narcissism and control. Control is certainly something that operated for his wife, whose training for the role as the hapless Christina in *Les Diaboliques* seems, in itself, a trifle diabolical. To get her into shape for the task of actor, Clouzot made her work for nine months learning parts from plays she would never act in but which he taped and then used to correct her delivery.[25] Interestingly, he had worked in a similar fashion with (his other novice) Montand for *Salaire*, for whom it clearly did work.[26] This is less evident in general terms for Vera Clouzot, whose tone of delivery is pretty monotone and movement very wooden. Although, having said that, it is also true that, because she behaves like a frozen and frightened rabbit caught in the headlights for most of the film, the terror she embodies works quite well against Signoret's unnerving, icy manner.

Finally, the secondary characters and especially the schoolchildren: Clouzot auditioned 300 children for the 35 he took. In among them he chose Jean-Philippe Smet (later to become known as Johnny Halliday), Yves-Marie Morin (Patrick Dewaere's brother, who plays Moinet) and Georges Poujouly of *Jeux interdits* fame (Clément, 1951), who plays Soudieu. The schoolmasters included a début part for Michel Serrault and, of course, a role for two stalwarts of Clouzot's oeuvre, Pierre Larquey as the vaguely dipsomaniac and well-named M. Drain (which literally means 'drain') and Noël Roquevert as the retired schoolmaster who, in part, inadvertently undermines the plot hatched by Michel and Nicole. Last but not least, Charles Vanel comes on board yet again, this time in the form of the somewhat decrepit retired Inspector Fichet.

The technical team

Les Diaboliques went into pre-production in early June 1954.[27] Production itself began in mid-July and the shooting was completed by the beginning of November. The film was shot on location and in studio. Clouzot discovered an abandoned chateau in Étang-la-Ville situated just beyond Saint-Cloud and the Bois de Boulogne, on the edge of the Forêt de Marly and en route to the National 12 – a convenient link onto the National 11, which takes

Nicole and Christina to Niort (some 360 kilometres south-west of Paris). Location shooting at Étang-la-Ville took up the first five of the 16-week shooting schedule. The derelict chateau matched perfectly Clouzot's need for a setting that spoke decay, dirt and decrepitude. The uncared-for building was consonant with the lack of care for the schoolboys, just as much as its decay implied the moral decrepitude of its adult inhabitants. The swimming pool was not only dirty and unused, again suggesting an uncaring, even unhealthy environment for the boys, but was also full of slime ('Thick as chocolate soup,' declares the brave Soudieu, who dives into the murky waters in an attempt to recover Nicole's keys). The sliminess undoubtedly points to the sleaziness of the teaching personnel – Christina excepted, of course. M. Drain is unkempt and sycophantic, M. Raymond looks to be following in his footsteps. Michel oozes nastiness and Nicole – if not exactly slimy – is far from inspiring trust. With regard to the two other locations (requiring two weeks' shooting), Clouzot scored a first with the one: the morgue scene is actually shot in a real mortuary.[28] As to the other, Clouzot could not resist a little tongue in cheek, to say nothing of auto-referentiality. Nicole's house is in Niort, Clouzot's birthplace. Furthermore, the actual house he used for the outside shots was located in Montfort-l'Amaury, directly opposite the house he used for his 'infamous' film *Le Corbeau* (almost as if he were cocking a snoot at the film censors and saying: 'Look, here I am again!').[29] The interiors were shot in the Saint-Maurice studios south-east of Paris and took an arduous nine weeks. The sets and interiors, with the exception (as we shall see) of Christina's bedroom, faithfully reproduced traditional boarding school spaces, provincial petit-bourgeois homes and modern Parisian hotels.

Camera, sets, lighting and sound are the absolute keys to the look of a Clouzot film. Clouzot's team of Armand Thirard (1899–1973), Léon Barsacq (1906–1969) and William-Robert Sivel (1908–1982) would work the magic for him on this film. Armand Thirard was Clouzot's favourite director of photography (he worked on seven of Clouzot's feature films). Thirard controlled the camera operators and, of course, the lighting. In working on *Les Diaboliques* he was presented with a more arduous task than usual. In order to speed up the already delayed shooting, Clouzot had two camera teams at work – both of whom had to be supervised by Thirard.[30] This explains why, when we read the credits, the names of three camera operators (rather than one) roll by, after Armand Thirard's, of course. This detailed naming was quite unusual as a general practice (at the time), but it points to the heaviness of the production practices and, as we know, Clouzot's target of 48 days' shooting was in the end doubled, despite having two teams. But, in all this, what is so remarkable is the great continuity in this film (in terms of lighting alone), achieved by the careful coordination put in place by Thirard. Equally remarkable is the seamless shift between location and studio lighting.

Thirard was 'a master of monochrome and colour, his interiors gave off a refulgence reminiscent almost of old Master paintings.'[31] As a master of monochrome, as this quote makes clear, he was obviously very aware of how to exploit source lighting, and this brings us back to Paul Meurisse's comment on the way Vera Clouzot and Simone Signoret were lit. In all the interior scenes, invariably, Vera Clouzot is fully lit, even highlighted, suggesting the use of considerable front lighting (as well as fill lights) because she looks quite white and is without any shadows on her face. On the contrary, Signoret is consistently held in neutral, even grey tones of light. Even the sequence when they are driving to Niort, where you might expect shifting light on the faces, produces no change. In fact, this scene was studio shot with back-projection. Once again it was possible to control light so that Vera Clouzot was in full light and Signoret in a grey shaded area. On the few occasions that there is sidelighting on Signoret's face, it is simply a case of levels of greyness and not of a contrastive black and white (as in an expressionist *chiaroscuro* shot, for example). Apart from the reasons for this practice supplied by Meurisse, that Clouzot was attempting to keep Signoret in the shadow of his wife, what this also does is to queer the picture for us as spectators. Let us assume we do not have the insider knowledge; how are we able to read this lighting of our two female protagonists – the bleached-white Christina and the grey Nicole? First of all, the lack of any true contrastive lighting on Signoret takes away from her potential role as a femme fatale. In her greyness, she hardly makes the mark, does she? Second, her grey is placed against Vera Clouzot's white, so here again she fails, this time to act as the negative (i.e. black) foil to Christina's supposed 'innocent, virginal' being. There is no positive and negative. Monochrome has been stripped of one of its salient features: its blackness. And this is where the twist comes in. Grey areas suggest a lack of clarity, as opposed to black – which, in the context of noir films, usually means bad, or the dark side of the self. The lighting on Signoret, then, signals to us that she is not what she seems; what it also tells us is that she is not a split persona (as the use of contrastive lighting on her *à la* film noir would have indicated to us). So, she remains more of a mystery to us than she would have done had she been constructed, through contrastive lighting, as a femme fatale or as a true villain. Nicole's interaction with the pupils in the science laboratory is another indication of her complex persona: here we see her ruffling Moinet's hair, showing at the very least a fondness for the young pupil (see picture on p. 23). Thus, Clouzot's attempts to shadow Signoret out into grey have had the opposite effect from the one he was trying to achieve; we are far more intrigued by this woman in grey than the woman in white. An interest Signoret keeps alive by the fluidity of her body as performance, as opposed to Vera Clouzot's stiff and wooden delivery. Signoret is a shadow that has made herself flesh.

But I want also to pause for a second on this question of monochrome versus colour in relation to Clouzot's film. By the mid-1950s colour and cinemascope were readily available, albeit expensive, formats. The cinemascope wide-screen process brought with it the magnetic soundtrack. As opposed to the optical mono soundtrack, the magnetic track provided high-fidelity sound and larger volume range as well as stereo-sound (seven- and four-track stereo was available). But its merits could be heard only on the new wide-screen format, thanks to the new quality projectors and sound system. However, exhibition practices at the time, for the most part, forestalled its use. Thus, very few theatres were equipped to run the new format given the expense of conversion. The advantages of magnetic sound were, however, felt at the post-production stage even for standard-format films, in that it was an easier system for mixing sound than the optical sound system and so helped to cut production costs.[32] Clouzot had hoped to shoot *Les Diaboliques* in cinemascope, while still keeping to black and white film.[33] This would have allowed him to profit fully from the merits of magnetic sound and to have made his film, sonorically speaking, even more terrifying. It was not the cost of cinemascope that held him back, however, but the effect on the image of projecting black and white cinemascope:

> I think it is very difficult to shoot a black and white film in cinemascope or vistavision because they are projected onto metallised screens which don't work with black and white. And I wasn't satisfied with the trials I had run with Technicolor. I don't want to shoot with so-called natural colours. I want to be able to work with colours that have been rendered.[34]

Interestingly, the debate around magnetic sound in the early 1950s was similar to that about colour. Both were seen as unrealistic. Until the mid- to late 1950s colour was still identified with films of fantasy and costume drama (not until the advent of colour television would it be deemed realistic). And because stereo sound did not 'speak from the screen' it was perceived as unrealistic in its spectacular effects. The effect of not using cinemascope meant, then, that at the time of *Les Diaboliques*' release its sound and standard format would, ultimately, vie in favour of realism for its audiences (black and white film with central optical sound being deemed more realistic). Spectators could have fear with conviction! And what is so fantastic about Clouzot's film is that – although it is, of course, a mono optical soundtrack – somehow, because of its density, it sounds almost as if it is in stereo. Using the Artec sound system he had to hand, his sound engineer, William-Robert Sivel, managed to make the soundtrack so loud at times that we feel our own ears hurting. This is especially true of the various sounds at the end of the film (the high-pitched squeaking doors, the thunderous clacking of the typewriter keyboard), which effectively send Christina tailspinning into a heart attack. The very opening credit sequence of the film – with the angelic voices of the

Nicole uncharacteristically showing fondness – ruffling Moinet's hair

boys' choir intoned over the credits contrasting heavily with the loud demonic music they are chanting – warns us that we are in for a painful and frightening experience.[35]

Sivel was a brilliant sound technician. He worked, in his lifetime, on over 300 films – nine of which were with Clouzot. And part of what made the soundtrack so special in its depth and resonance in *Les Diaboliques* was Sivel's ability to highlight the specific sounds Clouzot wanted to accentuate, through maintaining a virtual silence around them. Thus, we feel the terror entering Christina's heart as she hears the footsteps of her husband approaching the house in Niort. We listen to the tap dripping relentlessly on the nylon tablecloth as Christina, racked by guilt, is unable to sleep. We are warned early on in the film how much of a role the soundtrack has to play when we hear first the roar of the engine and then the wheels of the camionnette crushing the paper sailing boat left in a puddle. Every detail of the crunched paper and splash through the water is heard. The soundtrack, in other words, is as harsh and pitiless as the rest of the film.

The realism of the soundtrack depends, of course, on its ability to resonate properly within the decor. And the sets offered by Léon Barsacq admirably complement the sound; both gel into a sense of the real. It is surely no coincidence that Barsacq is credited as the 'architecte-décorateur' in this film – for his sets are those of an architect. He was a leading art director of his time, part of the wave of Russian émigrés who came to Paris during the 1920s. In Paris he trained in architecture and the decorative arts, much like Lazare Meerson before him (*the* poetic realist art director). He was assistant art director to Andrei Andrejew (a favourite of Clouzot's) and he worked with Alexander Trauner on Carné's *Les Enfants du paradis* (1944). Although trained up by some of the exemplary poetic realist set designers, Barsacq believed, like Meerson, that 'design should subordinate itself to the narrative, simply lending atmospheric support'.[36] Unlike the hyper-realist tendencies associated with poetic realist decor, therefore, Barsacq favoured a less complex design. He achieved a 'delicate balance between realism and artifice'[37] – something we can observe with his school interiors in *Les Diaboliques*, for example. The classrooms, refectory and dormitory are all completely consonant with boarding school spaces of that time (audiences would recognise and know them).

However, the private quarters of the school tell a different story and contrast quite shockingly with the sparseness of the rest of the school. The

Gothic richness of Christina's bedroom says more about her Latin American origins, her own inner psyche and devout Catholicism than it does about a mid-20-century boarding school headmistress's private quarters. It is actually quite intriguing that Michel should even agree to sleep in such a space, with its Catholicism oozing off the walls in the form of Christian icons and candles, to say nothing of the wooden palings carving up the space, making it more suggestive of a confessional box than a place of rest. While he certainly appears to rule the roost with an iron fist everywhere else in this nightmarish school, Michel has, to all intents and purposes, yielded to his wife's devoutly eccentric taste in the private sphere most readily associated with intimacy. Dare one suggest that the space smacks of femininity? As we shall see in the next chapter, Michel does not unambiguously or entirely occupy a masculine space. Indeed, much works within the narrative to place him in a more feminised one. This may help explain why, after everyone has left, he decides to rape his wife in the refectory rather than the bedroom. In any event, the oppressive decor of the bedroom suggests he is not as all-powerful as he at first might appear. And it is worth remembering that the only time he is in there is when he lies fast asleep in bed, fully dressed as if he had passed out in a drunken stupor, or (metaphorically) suffocated under the weight of the decor.

According to Barsacq,[38] getting the atmosphere right is what counts. He looks to find the atmosphere of each film and bring out the specific style that suits the period. To his mind, sets offer a précis of reality, not reality itself. This notion of précis suggests a lightness of touch, and indeed Barsacq's set designs were often produced in a sketch-like style which we associate with architectural design yet which, once put in place, have (as do real buildings) a material quality of the real – a quality helped, it has to be said, by the fact that Barsacq would always indicate the lighting effects. Barsacq's training in architecture is evident, then, in the dynamic composition of his sets, and we feel them breathing – although not necessarily fresh air, as we have noted in particular with Christina's stifling bedroom!

In a very similar way, objects in the film, particularly those that are held in extreme close-up, have an inherent power themselves, and it is instructive to note that the extreme close-up is not used at all until the terrorising of Christina in the last section of the film – at which point objects seem to come alive. Thing-power is something we associate with Hitchcock very readily.[39] Yet Clouzot is at least his equal. The first object that seems to take on a life of its own is the wicker trunk. When Nicole lets it go down the steps of the garage attic, it hurtles down the stairwell and almost takes Christina with it. Later, in Niort, it almost causes Christina to faint as she drags it across the hallway. At this point it is empty and we know that Nicole has had no problems moving it around, so its bulk works against Christina's fragility. Once the two women have bundled Michel's body into it and are trying, with M. Herboux' help, to get it into the camionnette, the trunk bursts a catch, exposing the plastic tablecloth inside, much like an overweight body bursting a button off and revealing the flesh beneath.[40] The trunk again threatens to expose the truth when the two women make a stop for petrol, and the pump attendant, having dragged the drunken soldier out of the back of their camionnette, notices a puddle of water. He assumes it is the soldier who has 'had an accident' and offers to wipe it up. Nicole, afraid that the secret will seep out, hurriedly slams the doors shut and takes off. Still the trunk has not finished having power. Right towards the end of the film Inspector Fichet discovers the trunk, which has now been returned to its original place, up in the garage attic, but which has tenaciously held onto a vital piece of evidence, namely the (still wet) plastic tablecloth. This secret is out.

Objects combine to stress Christina's ailing heart. The smallest of objects can have an effect. They have thing-power, which the use of sound and close-ups merely serves to intensify. Bathroom taps drip; plastic table-cloths hiss; clasps snap; Moinet's catapult moves about in mysterious ways, as does Michel's Prince of Wales suit; photographs reveal missing (presumed dead) husbands in the background; typewriters type away on their own; paper names names; and so on. Objects have almost corporeal substance. Conversely, human bodies (and hands) become unsubstantial shadows (especially Michel's). Objects make noise and have the ability to disappear and reappear with a randomness we more readily associate with human beings (in general, people move about, unlike inanimate objects, which do not move or generate sound unassisted). It is objects, rather than people, that make the unbelievable take on a life and become real, diabolical even. We are manipulated by them and their behaviour into suspending our disbelief, colluding with the terror they spawn.

Conclusion

Clouzot's love of the right detail goes across the whole spectrum of production. This obsession with the detail of the real – which he achieves through his intense pre-production planning and his ability to capitalise on the skills of his technicians – means that he creates a materially realist film that breathes its meaning. Terrifying sounds thunder from the centre of the screen and cause us to shy away, fearing the worst for our own hearts. The stifling decor of Christina's bedroom in which she finds herself entombed, the shocking whiteness of the bathroom that will never wash her clean of her 'crime' and in which she will perish – all this detail works to weave the sense of suffocating horror in which even we can no longer breathe.

Notes

1   *Edinburgh Film Festival Catalogue* 57, 2003, p. 123.
2   Pilard (1969), p. 109.
3   Bocquet (1993), p. 87.
4   Clouzot, quoted in Pilard (1969), p. 109.
5   See Barbey d'Aurevilly (1999), p. 49, which Clouzot slightly misquotes. Speaking of his short stories d'Aurevilly says: 'Elles [referring to *Diaboliques*] ont pourtant été écrites par un moraliste chrétien [...] qui croit que les peintres puissants peuvent tout peindre et que leur peinture est toujours assez *morale* quand elle est *tragique* et qu'elle donne *l'horreur des choses qu'elle retrace*/These stories have been written by a Christian moralist [...] who believes that powerful artists can paint everything and that their painting is always sufficiently *moral* when it is *tragic* and shows the *horror of the things it portrays*' (d'Aurevilly's emphasis).
6   See also Mayne, Judith (2000), pp. 49–50.
7   Bocquet (1993), p. 88.
8   Mayne (2001), p. 60.
9   Narcejac, quoted in Bocquet (1993), p. 88.
10   Clouzot, quoted in Bocquet (1993), p. 59.
11   Signoret (1978), p. 127.
12   Signoret (1978), p. 127, quoting Clouzot. This somewhat spiteful remark may be a question of sour grapes. After the war Clouzot had wanted to make *Casque d'or*, but in the end Jacques Becker got the go-ahead; Durant, Phillipe (1988), pp. 62–65.
13   Signoret (1978), p. 128.
14   Ibid., pp. 128–129.
15   Ibid., p. 129.
16   This situation was rendered all the more tense by the fact that for the last two weeks she was also rehearsing in Paris at the Théâtre Sarah Bernhardt for her

role as Elizabeth Proctor in the French adaptation of Arthur Miller's *The Crucible* (*Les Sorcières de Salem*, Raymond Rouleau). This meant rushing from the Saint-Maurice studios (outside Paris to the south-east) right back into the centre of town.

17   Signoret (1978), p. 128.

18   Paul Meurisse, quoted in Bocquet (1993), p. 90.

19   Interview with Meurisse by Durieux, Paulette, in *Télé 7-jours*, 8 October 1970, p. 32.

20   These details are provided by Bocquet (1993), p. 91. Apparently it took 11 takes to get it right; *Cinémonde*, 29 October 1954, p. 18.

21   Clouzot, quoted in Bocquet (1993), p. 89.

22   Clouzot, quoted in Pilard (1969), p. 61.

23   *Cinémonde*, 29 August 1954, p. 13 comments on how, in preparation for the role of Nicole, Signoret had to have her long, blonde hair cut off. Signoret tells us that her friends' reaction to it was positive, and that she too liked the new cut.

24   Clouzot, quoted in Pilard (1969), pp. 109–110.

25   Bocquet (1993), p. 89.

26   Hamon and Rotman (1990), pp. 276–277.

27   *Le Film français*, 4 June 1954, p. 16.

28   *Cinémonde*, 28 January 1955, p. 13 supplies this information.

29   *Cinémonde*, 3 December 1954, p. 16.

30   *Cinémonde*, 28 January 1955, pp. 12–13 is the source for these various tidbits of productionalia.

31   Quoted from Armand Thirard's 'Filmography', in *Focus on Film* 13, Special, 1973, p. 72 (no author provided).

32   See Belton, John, (1992), 'Magnetic sound: the frozen revolution', in R. Altman (ed.), *Sound Theory, Sound Practice*, New York and London, Routledge, pp. 154–167. Belton gives a very full and illuminating analysis of this new technology and its impact.

33   Bocquet (1993), p. 90.

34   Clouzot, quoted in Bocquet (1993), p. 90.

35   Georges Van Parys scored the music for this opening sequence. Previously he had scored music for *Casque d'or* – musically an entirely more melodic and gentle affair.

36   Votolato, Gregory (2000), p. 66.

37   Ibid., p. 66.

38   Barsacq, Léon (1970), p. 70.

39   I am indebted to Jane Bennett for this expression 'thing-power', which she first presented in a seminar paper at Exeter University in October 2003. See her article 'The force of things: steps toward an ecology of matter', in *Political Theory* 32 (3), 2004, pp. 347–372.

40   It took ten takes to get this scene right. Apparently, each time Signoret lifted the trunk, she did so with such vigour it looked as if she were lifting a hatbox. Yet it had a live person in it to give realism and weight; *Cinémonde*, 3 December 1954, p. 16.

2   Plot, camera, characterisation

Plot structure

The plot of *Les Diaboliques* revolves around the fact that a body has gone missing – one which is no longer there (as indeed the original title, *Celle qui n'était plus*, makes clear although in the context of the film it becomes 'celui', namely the husband). Two women (a wife and mistress) plot to murder (through drowning) a detestable man who tyrannises them both. All appears to go to plan. The man is murdered and tossed into a filthy swimming pool. So far so good. But the next day the body cannot be found. The pool is emptied and, to the wife's horror, the dead man has disappeared. The shock almost kills her. But she recovers, only to be further assailed by evidence that her dead husband must still be alive. His suit turns up from the dry-cleaners. When she and the mistress go to question the owner of the dry-cleaning business, she helps their investigation move forward by supplying a hotel key left behind in the suit pocket. The husband, it appears, has rented himself a little pied-à-terre in the fashionable 17th arrondissement of Paris. When the two women turn up at his hotel, however, he remains as invisible as ever.[1] Things look to be resolved when a newspaper article announces that a naked body has been found in the river Seine. The wife sets off to the morgue to identify her husband successfully (she hopes). To no avail: it is not him. More shocks to her system. By now the original desire to get rid of her husband is turning into a nightmarish attempt to find his body. To top it all, a retired police inspector has pushily joined in, uninvited, to help investigate the disappearance. The wife, increasingly riddled by remorse and fear, banishes the mistress. The inspector gradually works out what has happened, but too late to save the wife, as it transpires. She dies, diabolically driven to her death by the – at first – ghostly and – subsequently – all too real evidence (as in the body returns alive) that her husband is not dead after all.

Structurally, *Les Diaboliques* can be neatly divided into four parts – as the following diagram makes clear:

Diagram 1 – Plot structure

Part One	Part Two	Part Three	Part Four
Setting the scene: the school; the triangular relationship Michel/ Christina/Nicole	Leaving for Niort; 'murder'; return to school; dumping body in swimming pool; things go according 'to plan'	The body disappears; Nicole and Christina investigate; things are not going according 'to plan'	Christina goes to the morgue; Inspector Fichet comes along and investigates; the real plan/plot is uncovered
Michel is in charge	Nicole is in charge	First Nicole, then Christina is in charge	Inspector Fichet is in charge
Duration: 16m47s	*Duration:* 38m	*Duration:* 21m	*Duration:* 37m51s

In terms of who appears to be in control, as we can see, the two women, between them, are in charge during the central part (parts two and three) of the narrative for a duration of 59 minutes. However, the plot is structured in such a way that men – either Michel or Inspector Fichet – bookend the narrative and are in control for a duration of 54 minutes and 38 seconds. With hindsight, however, Michel's control is very quickly brought into question by the occurrences in part two. Thus, he is less the master of the moment than he appeared to be at first. His power is seemingly diminished quite quickly within the narrative – undermined, in fact, by the women (and their plot to kill him). Indeed, of the men, it is only Fichet who has the ability to restore law and order, not Michel – who, as it transpires, is solely an agent of disruption. It is, after all, his greed for Christina's money and his lust for Nicole that drive him to commit the crime of terrorising his wife to death. The central part of the film is interesting, however, for a number of structural reasons. For a start, it is rare in French film noir for women to have such a dominant role – especially one that is virtually equal in length to that of the men. Notably, however, their power, as we shall learn in the end, is all associated with illusion. The female dominance, then, is undermined by the outcome. For, as we discover, once Fichet starts to investigate and uncover the truth, the women have in fact committed a non-murder and are, as a result, investigating a non-mystery (since there is no missing body, only a missing, alive Michel). In a sense, they are expending fruitless energy; their quest has no purpose. Thus, their control is as spurious and as much of a simulacrum as Michel's appeared to be in part one. Everyone, with the exception of Fichet, is playing to false situations of control – some with knowledge (Nicole and Michel), some without (Christina). Furthermore, the issue of Michel's agency in part one comes full circle again. As we find out at the end, he was playing dumb to the situation in part one (pretending not to know that the two women were plotting, even though he knew exactly what was happening). So he did, in the end, have some form of control then. However, his problem is that, while he might be smart enough (with Nicole's help) to outwit Christina, he is not cunning enough to outfox the older crusty patriarch.

Christina dies only half understanding the truth: that her husband is not dead despite the fact that she had killed him. Nothing leads us to believe that she has worked out that it was a dastardly plot concocted by Nicole and Michel to bring about her death. Given her Catholicism and belief in the supernatural, a return from the dead could just be possible. Even if that is too farfetched, nonetheless, her conscience works to her downfall. Christina's traumatic dream at the end of the film, from which she awakens to find Fichet (the embodiment of the law) looming over her, serves only to confirm her realisation that she is condemned for the rest of her life to bear witness to the murder. Her last moments alive are invested in confirming her guilt. She *has* to trace the source of the footsteps she hears and the shadow she has seen. By finding the 'live corpse' she hopes to put an end to the traumatic event of Michel's dying. However, there is no way out; alive or dead, he will constantly remind her of her criminal deed. To find him alive means she is condemned to one set of traumatic repetitions, just as surely as she is condemned to another set of traumatic nightmares if he remains dead. The only way of ending it is to end herself, to die. To abrogate power completely.

Equally significant in relation to this notion of the undermining of female power is the fact that, even during the period when the two women are in charge, the male still manages to intrude and risk exposing their crime. When in Niort to carry out the murder, the retired schoolteacher notes down the time of both the running of the bathwater and its draining away (a vital set of clues that, when the two schemers are brought to court, will surely serve to uncover their plot); then, of course, there is his clumsy handling of the trunk (already mentioned) and the drunken soldier who climbs into the back of the camionnette. Small wonder that Nicole is so sharp and rude to them all and just about keeps them at bay. But the female control is precarious at best, and the last male to intrude, Inspector Fichet, is the one who successfully manages to get under the net (or the plastic tablecloth) of what is, after all, an illusion and expose it for what it is: a contemptible hoax.

Curiously, in the original novel, female dominance is not undermined. Lucienne remains the dominant figure throughout the narrative and the husband, Ravinel, a weak exploitable creature. The entire scheme in the novel, to defraud the insurance company, is hers. Ravinel (unaware that it is his life that is in danger and believing it is his wife's life insurance they will get) follows meekly along with the plan. In fact, he still feels considerable fondness for his wife, Mireille, so the scheme to murder her purely for the money seems less convincing than the murder plot in the film. A first shift in meaning occurs then. In the film we are not in the know as to the real plot; we do not realise that greed is at the bottom of it all. Thus, we take at face value that Nicole and Christina are not motivated by gain in their plot to kill Michel. Indeed, this absence of pecuniary motive makes their desire to be rid of him both plausible and seemingly rational. At first we might experience some sympathy for them, because Michel is so cruel. Not so the characters in the novel; they are all quite unappetising from the start. As to the question of female dominance, the retired inspector, Inspector Merlin, who offers to help Ravinel trace his wife does not have the persistence of his filmic recreation, Inspector Fichet. Indeed, he rather summarily dismisses Ravinel's evidence as hallucinations and leaves him to it. Thus, the women outwit the men. Not only that, their lesbian relationship is the one that is allowed to survive: the women get their hands on the money and take off to Antibes. Their crime does pay, but only because Ravinel, a pitiful male, embodies a type of masculinity that was so much in evidence at that time, both in noir literature and noir realist films – namely, a masculinity in crisis (which even the institutional voice of the law rejects, in the person of Inspector Merlin!).

For Nicole and Michel, however, crime does not pay. And there are a number of reasons for this. The reversal of the narrative by Clouzot causes several interesting things to occur. Michel, for a start, occupies a far more complex situation than Ravinel. Essentially, as the ostensible murder victim, he gets to occupy the narrative position formerly assigned to Mireille. Yet he is also an extremely virile male, prone to aggressive and domineering ways. And money drives his desire to get rid of Christina. In all these ways, he takes on Lucienne's behavioural traits. The traits he most assuredly does not espouse are those of Ravinel, the original husband. In other words, on two counts he is associated with the two female personas of the novel: the strong, masculine Lucienne and the weak, feminine Mireille. As I shall argue later (in Chapter 3), Michel occupies in part the position of the femme fatale, but we can already see here how that is the case. He is both cruel and manipulative (like Lucienne); later, he is reduced to a floppy feminised weakness by the spiked whisky he drinks and, once he disappears, becomes the object of investigation (as Mireille does in the novel, and like all femme fatales in film noir). Nicole also occupies in part the role of the femme fatale – though not, as we shall see, with as much conviction as Michel. But this overlapping queers the narrative pitch, so to speak – the trope or stereotype of the femme fatale becomes too fragmented. Who is the femme fatale here? Answering this question is not helped by the fact that Nicole, like Michel, has many traits in common with Lucienne: she has a murky past, her face is hard and implacable, she is ruthless and manipulative.[2] But here similarities draw to a halt. Nicole's femme fataleness slips into a rather parochial petite bourgeoisie. Whereas Lucienne and Michel are obsessed with money, Nicole is obsessively mean. She gives full display to this when she is in Niort: she insists on turning out the lights once the shutters are open so as not to be wasteful; she complains about the price of the whisky she buys to put the sleeping draught in; she is furious at the cost of the plastic tablecloth bought to shroud Michel in once he is drowned; she is so mean she has not replaced the ageing bathpipes in her house. It is her meanness more than her cold, manipulative ways that gives her away in the end. No glamorously devious and slinky femme fatale behaviour here, then – merely sordid meanness. Because she is such a cheapskate, the plastic tablecloth is of poor quality, and tears. Water leaks out in the camionnette and is discovered later by Inspector Fichet in the wicker trunk hidden back up in the garage attic; as a result of this discovery he works out how the murder was carried out.

Throughout the novel it is as if Lucienne and Ravinel are working against each other. Lucienne stays as far away as possible from the crime scene – she works in Nantes and Ravinel lives just outside Paris – and she expects Ravinel to do all the dirty work. She is merely the brains behind the crime and, as such, she is almost as much of a ghost as Mireille. Once the murder has happened Ravinel for his part becomes consumed by guilt and terrified by the hauntings of his wife, whom he now realises he really quite loved. Lucienne dominates from afar, but such is her power, that both Ravinel and Mireille commit the act of murder for her – Mireille to end her boring existence with Ravinel, Ravinel because he has allowed himself to be manipulated by Lucienne into believing this is what he wants. Yet, unlike Michel, he neither hates nor abuses his wife. He collapses and dies in a state of penitence – longing for his old life back. The point of the novel is to reveal the impotence of men in the face of scheming and independent women who no longer need them. A new kind of criminality, that of the lesbian predator, is portrayed as something unfamiliar, uncanny and which threatens, but against which there is little defence since it is so 'unknowable'. And because it is unknowable, this time, crime pays. In the end it could be argued that the novel points more truthfully to the unease felt around female sexuality in the 1950s – its uncontainability after the war – than does the film. This is not to claim, however, that Clouzot was reticent around taboo subjects. As Judith Mayne makes clear,[3] he has consistently foregrounded questions of sexuality and gender in his films. For example, in his earlier film, *Quai des Orfèvres*, he introduced the lesbian figure of Dora who did not figure in the original novel. She is a sympathetic character who is not in any way judged for her sexual preferences and who ends up commanding the respect of the police inspector. And, indeed, even if, in *Les Diaboliques*, Clouzot felt the need to straighten out the story for his wife Vera's sake, nonetheless the queer – as we shall see – still creeps in. Arguably for Clouzot, on the face of things, the primary focus this time was on the complexity of making the thriller work differently through a creative play with the signs rather than an overt discourse on questions of sexuality. Thus, suspense comes to the fore and sexuality moves to the backburner. There is no need for plot line to carry a great burden of representation since the purpose of the film is to make a spine-chilling thriller.

The film, then, is not about masculinity in crisis, although it does, almost despite itself, reveal the unfixity of gender. By heterosexualising the story, Clouzot makes the plot one of the oldest in the book: getting rid of the wife so the mistress and husband can make off with the money. And this is why their crime does not pay: the imperative of film noir logic dictates that they must get found out. How long Clouzot can keep us from finding out is the trick of the film and its source of suspense. Nicole and Michel, as we learn by the end of the film, have worked together fantastically as a team, like clockwork. Both Nicole and Michel are the metteurs-en-scène of the plot to 'kill off' Christina, and so they equal each other in their cruelty. This is not the case for the original couple: it is Lucienne alone who is hard as nails (exemplified by the fact that she is constantly filing her fingernails with vigour). Ravinel is soft and weak, certainly not cruel. Nicole and Michel also equal each other in their incredible meanness. Michel's stinginess, as exemplified in the revolting food he provides for the pupils, is completely unforgivable – as indeed Christina at one point tells him. Nicole's penny-pinching – while it might find some external rationale in the effects of the post-war mentality of never wasting anything – nonetheless is deeply unattractive. They remain two sides of a gendered coin therefore – unlike Lucienne and Ravinel, who in terms of gender stereotypes switch over roles (she is masculine, he emasculated and quite feminine). But (as we shall also see) Michel and Nicole constitute two sides of the femme fatale coin – arguably to the extent that their power cancels each other out. As such, neither of them occupies the space of masculinity in crisis in the way that Ravinel does. But they do foreground a complex set of questions around gender and sexuality that surprisingly, the original novel given its lesbian intertext, merely touches upon.

Camerawork

Shot distribution reveals how Clouzot constructs his tight thriller. Shot predominantly in medium shot and close-up, the effect is a claustrophobic atmosphere. Reinforcing this sense of stifling anxiety is the increased density of shots per minute. At 6.5 shots per minute, the shooting speed in this film is faster than the average for a French film (the average, at the time, varying between 4.4 and 5.5 per minute).[4] The percentages of shots are as follows:

Diagram 2 – Percentage of shots

Long shots	Medium shots	Medium close-ups	Close-ups	Extreme close-ups
4%	27%	39%	29%	1%

(mcu, cu, ecus = 69%)

Note the intensity of close-up shooting – well over half of the film (69%). And if we look at the distribution of the shots over the four parts, then further intriguing data emerges:

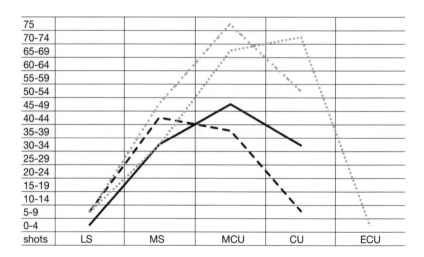

We can observe how parts one and three follow a similar graphic movement in terms of peaking at around the 45 mark, flattening off and then falling; whereas parts two and four peak much higher, around the 75 mark, and then fall off. This suggests greater levels of intensity and, indeed, claustrophobia in parts two and four, created by the significant rise in MCUs and CUs. And, if we consider the patterns overall, then what emerges is that parts one and three, in their less extreme shape, act as foils to parts two and four, respectively. In other words, they build up the momentum, setting the scene for the other two, more explosive parts. Thus, parts one and three are where Clouzot cranks up, begins to wind up the mechanism that will be let loose in all its ferocity in the murder sequence (in part two) and the terrorising of Christina (in part four).

The most balanced shape is in part one, as one would expect, since it establishes the various relationships. The three other parts are similar in that the MCUs or CUs outnumber the MSs. This intensification in tight framing matches the thriller nature of the film. So all these shapes make considerable sense. However, what is intriguing is that the fastest paced of all four parts is part one, at 7.4 shots per minute. The three other parts are quite even in nature: 6.2, 6.5 and 6.2, respectively. Thus, a series of questions immediately arise. Why the fast early pace of part one? Why the even pacing in the rest? Why intensify the shots and not the pace at the same time? And here it is that I believe we come to Clouzot's love of tensions and paradoxes. We know he pre-planned his films meticulously, so there is nothing arbitrary in the above rhythms we have noted.

A first obvious reason for the fast pacing of part one comes down to the number of characters Clouzot has to introduce. But, if we recall that six different locations or sets get used here, then we can understand more about this pacing. Two sequences in this first part are exteriors, the other three are interiors. In them we get a feel for the topography of the different, individual spaces: the school playground, the swimming pool, the corridors, science lab, refectory and Christina's bedroom. But we do not yet know fully how they all link up. In other words, the mapping or geography of the space is not yet completely clear. The fast pacing then muddles us a little with regard to the real space we are looking at. And this will become significant only in the last sequence of the film (when Christina dies). The speed, then, of this first part works to introduce both characters and space but it also serves to reveal less than more – speed as a sleight of hand (or camera) is what is at work here. As to the even pacing of the other three parts of his film, here Clouzot creates the feeling that something inexorable is about to happen. It is like a hanging sense of doom – the longer it gets drawn out the more even-tempoed it is and the more threatening it feels. The shots provide a sense of cranking up the intensity of pain while the pacing evokes a progressive, measured suffocation.

Even the panning and tracking shots, of which there are many, fail to bring any air into this stifling and cruel atmosphere. Given that there is, on average, one tracking shot per minute and one pan every two, we could hope to feel less fixed. But such is not the case. All the tracking shots are quite short, some even remarkably so. At times the tracking shot gets interrupted, stopped in its tracks, as it were, before being able to pick up again. At other times this stop-start feel becomes almost a rocking back and forward, with a backtracking being almost immediately followed by a forward-tracking. This is particularly the case in the murder scene in Nicole's apartment, especially if we measure from the moment Michel arrives until he is drowned. A quarter of the shots in that sequence are in tracking (21 out of 84 shots). There are ten forward- and 11 backtracking shots. A sense of buffeting occurs (reminding us of Clouzot's boxing analogy once more), and we are quite right to feel somewhat unstable. This feeling is compounded by the fact that, taking the film as a whole, there are twice as many backtracking shots as forward ones (71 to 37), to say nothing of the fact that most of them are in either MS or MCU. We can easily feel ourselves falling back into some unidentified hole since we have no idea what is behind us. A diabolical vertigo if ever there was one!

Characterisation

In terms of characterisation, there are numerous reflections and refractions between individuals and groups of individuals. Thus, almost in hierarchical fashion, the initial triangle between Michel, Nicole and Christina is reflected by the second-order characters M. Drain, M. Raymond and Plantiveau, and subsequently by M. and Mme Herboux. To explain: Drain and Raymond are immediate foils for Michel and Nicole. The hypocrisy, snideness, lack of compassion for the schoolboys and general nastiness of the adulterous couple

(Michel and Nicole) finds an easy echo in Drain and Raymond's own behaviour. M. Raymond and M. Herboux' know-it-all behaviour is a mirroring of Nicole's own need to assert her knowledge (on a couple of occasions she asserts the superiority of her knowledge over Drain and Raymond). Christina, for her part, finds a ready mirroring in Plantiveau, the man who is kind and concerned when it comes to the well-being of the schoolboys. He too is worried about the poor quality of their nutrition, but is as ineffectual as Christina in getting Michel to change his mean ways. M. and Mme Herboux, living upstairs in the Niort house, are mirror images of the strange couple – Nicole and Christina – below. M. Herboux, like Nicole, is bossy and domineering; he insists that he knows best, reacts angrily when thwarted, is crisp and sharp in both his speech and movements, and unceremoniously expects to have his way all the time (as, for example, when he bangs his shoe on the floor), in the same way that Nicole brusquely commandeers her pupils out of their classroom, tosses the rubber at Christina, and so on. Mme Herboux, like Christina, so clearly lives in her husband's shadow. As if to make this point all the clearer there is a moment, as she opens the door to Nicole, when all we see is her shadow projected onto the wall opposite the door. Mme Herboux is weak and subservient and one cannot imagine her standing up to her tyrannical husband any more than we can Christina to hers – or, indeed, to Nicole.

The children play an interesting role in the film. They are certainly not represented as some ideal of innocence, as opposed to the Manichean ways of their elders. But their naturalness is contrasted with the more extreme behaviour of the grown-ups. The boys exude normalcy: they joke about sex, they cannot wait to achieve puberty and so start shaving early, they tell half-truths, perhaps even lies, they misbehave in the refectory because the food is so awful. Yet, despite the meanness of the school director, they remain exuberant, willing to please, wanting to shine in front of their favourite teacher (Christina, of course). So, as such, they act as a third-order foil to the first and second triangular relationships. They do not, however, mirror their elders but refract against their image, showing how limited and distorted it is and how venal and pusillanimous their elders are. The ending, when Moinet asserts that he has seen Christina (although everyone knows she is dead), acts as a kind of coda on the film. The last word is with the schoolboy, and can be read in several ways. First, that, because of the corrupting ways of their elders, he has learned to lie so well he cannot distinguish between truth and fiction. Second, it answers back to the opening score of the film when the angelic voices of the schoolboys intone a sinister and diabolical chant, suggesting that education is more monstrous than it is enlightening (a reading supported by the terrible system of rote-learning we hear being chanted out, from time to time, by the pupils). Finally, and most sadly, Moinet is experiencing the first stages of grief (denial), which none of his elders can recognise; unable to recognise emotions for what they are, they decide he must be punished. There is something quite gruesomely cruel in sending the youngster to the corner of a now completely abandoned and doubly derelict school – not just physically derelict but morally so, thanks to the teachers' dereliction of their pastoral and pedagogical duties.

Notes

1   Much of this plot (of being absent but apparently living) is played out in a not dissimilar fashion in Hitchcock's 1959 *North by Northwest*.
2   See Boileau, Pierre and Narcejac, Thomas (1952), pp. 36, 52, 54, 57 and 63 for descriptions of Lucienne that equally match Nicole.
3   Mayne (2000), p. 60.
4   *Les Diaboliques* has 737 shots over 114 minutes.

3   Texts and intertexts: what kind of film is this – noir, queer, political?

Les Diaboliques is something of an unsettled text. In the previous chapter I suggested various reasons linked to the nature of the adaptation, and this chapter will further explore this unsettledness. But let us first consider its generic pedigree. When released in France it was labelled as a psychological thriller, which of course it is. But it is also more. In fact, it marks a *point tournant* in the history of the French thriller, in that, arguably, it can be seen as *the* French film noir to end all French films noirs (of the post-war period, anyway). As such, it represents a climax to the noir tradition in France (which began in the 1930s) and is a film that, in its intelligence and playful duping of the audience, set new boundaries for this generic tradition and gave pause for thought to Hollywood film noir directors (most significantly Hitchcock). This and the next chapter will go on to demonstrate this. But, first, what is particularly important here is to make clear how the French noir is distinct from its American counterpart. This in turn will allow us to see, in our analysis, how much Clouzot's text adheres to, yet resists, the French model.

Historically, and arguably, French noir predates American noir. Films of the French poetic realist tradition of the late 1930s were black pessimistic films and have, with hindsight, been considered as one of the precursors to noir films. And, even though the actual term 'film noir' is generally accepted as a post-constructed category[1] used to refer to the American thriller and tough gangster films of the 1940s and 1950s, in fact, as Ginette Vincendeau points out, these French late 1930s films were the first to be 'routinely' labelled 'film noir' by film critics.[2]

Although there is some overlap in the visual style, tone and narrative of the American and French noirs, the actual literary sources of the scenarios help point to a first difference. In the main, the major influence for American noir was hard-boiled crime or detective fiction. But the 1940s American noir was also deeply influenced by Hollywood's popularisation of Freudian psychoanalysis. As Krutnik explains, 'Psychoanalytic terms and therapeutic practices [had] gradually made inroads into many areas of American cultural life' as a result of the effects of the first World War, and 'by the 1940s (exacerbated once more by wartime psychoneurotic disorders) a popularised version of psychoanalysis had become entrenched in Hollywood's productions.'[3] Thus, in adapting hard-boiled pulp fiction, American noir products tended to focus on both criminal activity and the psychological breakdown and sexual malaise of the central male protagonist.[4] With this sexual malaise came, of course, a concomitant anxiety surrounding the female. During the war period, women had found fulfilment outside the traditional family unit. This, in turn, led to a hostility towards women, which, in the noir context, gets reflected as a mixture of fear and fascination that the hero 'projects onto her'.[5] Thus, the femme fatale is born out of the hero's conflicting desires, and it is she who wields power over him. She becomes the threat to his masculinity, as he desperately tries to ascertain whether she can be trusted or not – an ambivalence that makes him vulnerable and, in equal measure, sexually paranoid.

Arguably, the French were ahead of the Americans in this psychological domain as well. For, in terms of parallels with American noir, it was the poetic realist films that presented us with such deeply angst-ridden (often working-class) heroes whose psychological frailty seemed fatalistically to lead them to their death (often by suicide). Masculinity was in crisis here as France faced yet another threat of war – its ineluctability being the darkness that confronted all young men. And often the woman was part of the fatalistic trap that would lead the hero to his demise.

In the French context, and in terms of the thriller film (also known as the *polar*), crime literature was (as for the American noir) a major source, beginning in the 1930s with Georges Simenon's adaptations of his Maigret novels – a source that still endures today. However, Maigret is a very different prospect from the tough private eyes or detectives of American pulp fiction. In his middle-agedness, his love of good food, his ability not to move but reflect on and process information gathered from witnesses to solve the enigma, Maigret is almost the exact opposite of his American noir counterpart. Later, after the war, Simenon continued to be an influence, but other writers came on the scene with their psychological crime thrillers. Emblematic of these writers are the authors Sébastien Japrisot, Pierre Boileau and Thomas Narcejac. Boileau and Narcejac were a two-man team that was extremely successful, with close on 50 titles to their names, 12 of which were made into films (including, as we know, *Celle qui n'était plus/Les Diaboliques* and *D'entre les morts/Vertigo*).

Ginette Vincendeau has called these post-war French noir films 'social noir' films.[6] This is a useful distinction, in my view, since the product is indeed more varied than the American prototype, in that, while it contains noir elements, it also transcends it. Thus, as Vincendeau points out, in its noirness the French product is seemingly not unlike its American brother. The settings are urban, the photography uses contrastive black and white, the narratives are pessimistic, pitting the troubled male protagonist either against his past or some treacherous woman. But where it does differ is on at least three counts. First, spectatorial pleasure is derived as much from watching the star-protagonist as it is from 'social voyeurism'.[7] Second, although she is often the one who leads the men to their demise, the femme fatale in French noir, especially after the war, is nonetheless a much reduced figure in relation to her American sister, and lacks the latter's over-ridingly dangerous 'erotic charge'.[8] Indeed, Vincendeau argues that the French femme fatale all but disappears after the war, leaving greater space for the men.[9] In terms of spatial dynamics far greater attention is paid to the moral ambiguity of the male than to any psychological (or other) *mise en scène* of the woman character. Finally, the social noir, as its label suggests, is socially 'anchored'[10] – and as such it does two things: on the one hand, it speaks to the aftermath of the war and the humiliating effects of the occupation of France by the Germans, and, on the other, it reflects very realistically the harsh socio-economic climate of the times.

Clouzot's film becomes interesting when viewed in this light because we can see how mould-breaking he was. In the first instance, he makes two women the centre of his narrative. Michel is fairly marginalised, at least physically – yet, as we shall see, he comes to occupy an interesting position within the triangular relationship. Furthermore, he is far from being morally

ambiguous. We know he is horrid from the start. And, in terms of psychological angst, it is not he but his wife who is riddled with anxiety and guilt. In
the second instance, it becomes increasingly difficult, during the unravelling
of the plot, to know how to locate the femme fatale. To all intents and
purposes it looks as if Nicole should be the one to embody that role. But
this reading of her as femme fatale is a very difficult one to make the first
time we see the film. Because her game is a double masquerade we are
unable to interpret her actions as treacherous. We are not aware until the
very end that, through pretending to lead the man to his demise, she is in
fact leading the other woman to hers. To complicate matters further, in this
context of trying to fix Nicole as the femme fatale – which, in a sense, we can
do only when we have seen the entire film – there are times (as we shall see)
when, even if she is supposed to be the femme fatale, she seems deliberately
to evacuate that role. Rather than eliminate the femme fatale, however,
Clouzot appears to fragment her at will: it could be any one of these three
central characters. And it is this shifting uncertainty that is such a hallmark
of Clouzot's thriller/noir films and that keeps us, the audience, in such a
state of unease. Similarly, when it comes to social voyeurism, Clouzot reveals
to us the ugly connivance and mean-spiritedness of the bourgeoisie, but he
does not allow us to contemplate it at our leisure. We are pulled and twisted
around in this domain also, partly because we are unable or unsure as to
whom we should identify with, and partly because the realism with which
he portrays the microcosmic society of the boarding school is so convincing
we feel tainted by its dank and sordid atmosphere.

   With regard to the primary triangle in this thriller narrative (Michel,
Nicole and Christina), something very queer is going on. And it comes
down to this fundamental question: who and where is the femme fatale?
Traditionally, the expectation would be that the femme fatale would occupy
the apex. Clearly, this is not exclusively the case; in male-centred films noirs
the hero victim will be the camera's focus. But to return to our femme fatale.
She would be the chief object of scrutiny. Alternatively, the murdered body, or
vanished body (as long as it too is female), can be at the top of the triangle and
the object of prurient investigation (in this context Otto Preminger's *Laura*,
1944, is a classic). Finally, in these generalisations, the wife either plays a very
secondary role or is the victim, and as such disappears quite early on, or is
sometimes but rarely the femme fatale. In *Les Diaboliques*, Christina occupies

none of these positions. She is certainly not the femme fatale, nor is she the murdered wife (even though she falls victim to a heart attack at the very end). Yet it is she who is primarily at the apex. As explained in Chapter 1, she dominates the shots. Let us look in more detail in the following diagram:

Diagram 3 – Distribution of solo shots

	Signoret/Nicole	Clouzot/Christina	Meurisse/Michel
Close-up	3	9	4
Medium close-up	15	51	16
Medium shot	41	35	24
Long shot	13	26	0
Totals	72	121	44

If Nicole is the femme fatale then there is an unexpected inversion in terms of the ratio of close-ups to medium and long shots (1:3). Compare this with Christina, who has as many close-ups as she does medium and long shots (giving a ratio of 1:1). And what about Michel? He is, proportionately speaking, more often in close-up than Nicole. He comes out with a percentage of 45% (Nicole's is 33%), which brings him closer to Christina's 50%. Furthermore, with regard to the ratio of close-ups to medium and long shots, he again comes closer to Christina, with a figure of 2.5:3 (almost 1:1). Of the three characters, Nicole is the one who occupies the least feminised of the positions in relation to the camera and therefore, in terms of the conventions of the genre, is actually the most unlikely of the three as a candidate for the role of femme fatale. I am well aware that some American femmes fatales are played by 'masculinised' stars (e.g. Barbara Stanwyck and Joan Crawford). But they remain the central focus *and* their masculinisation is part of the conceit of fetishising the female body to contain her as safe. The point here is that, although Signoret is masculinised, she manages to annul the fetishising process by evacuating the position of femme fatale. And, in so doing, she queers the pitch.

Indeed, in terms of shots, Michel occupies almost as strongly a female position as Christina. Yet, here again, things are at odds. For Christina is as much in evidence, if not more, in medium and long shots as is Nicole (Nicole on 56 and Christina on 61) – a position of activity which suggests an equal involvement on her part to Nicole's in moving the plot along and which also suggests that both (albeit at different times) essentially occupy the role that traditionally should have been that of Paul Meurisse's character. Both women, then, have parity here, and we recall that in part three it is Christina who takes over control (becomes the investigating agent). Thus, Christina does not unambiguously occupy the apex of the triangle – nor, indeed, any exclusively female space. The evidence here is that she is not as weak and passive as we at first might believe. Conversely, Michel is greatly feminised, and this is quintessentially underlined by the fact that it is his disappearance, his enigma, that gets investigated. Thus, rather than participating in anything that could be qualified as action-packed masculinity in practice, he takes on the role more traditionally associated with the femme fatale in film noir: namely, the body as an object of fascination and scrutiny. He thereby usurps the place that should have been that of the female lead. Michel's passivity and feminisation – which begins by his being the 'victim' who is murdered and then continues as he remains the invisible subject – is strongly counter-balanced by Nicole's no-nonsense practicalities. She occupies – not necessarily by default, either, given her short-cropped hair and her rather unsexualised clothing – an overarching masculinised space that is greater than that of the other two. Her dress barely changes throughout the film and the cut is consistently the same. She either wears a pencil-line dress or a daytime functional tunic-styled dress that can be belted to give a certain severe elegance or, if left unbelted (as it is later on in the film) to be worn for comfort.[11] We note that she has no painted fingernails. The only elements that hint at an iconicity of femme fatale are her sunglasses and her high heels, and even these she quickly shelves in favour of carpet slippers as soon as she can, as if disinclined to inhabit such a prescriptive space (as that of the femme fatale).

Nicole's evacuating of her role as femme fatale causes a disruption within the narrative and it is as if the strength of her characterisation permits the original text to bleed back in, permitting a queer reading. As an effect of heterosexualising the text, Les Diaboliques confronts us with sexualities that fail to run true to type or refuse almost to conform with the film noir generic narrative's expectation of them. In a 'normal' film noir, while the femme fatale leads the man (who is weak in flesh) to his doom, we do at least sense his passion for her. Here all we get is the appearance of a trap being set, but one in which both women collude. They are, after all, using the pretence of the threat of divorce to get Michel to Niort – so in a sense the death of passion (Christina's) is driving the narrative here far more than any intrigue about money on the women's part. Furthermore, we sense no desire between Michel and Nicole, merely cruel brutality on one side and icy indifference on the other. There is, then, a mismatch, in this film, between sex and gender and, ultimately, desire – the last of which appears to have been completely erased at the heterosexual level, in any event. Thus, we are presented with incoherencies that have the converse effect of the desired outcome (nothing in the straight context rings true), and, as such, it is heterosexuality that in the final analysis is destabilised. Indeed, what fire there is in this film firmly lies between the two women.

Let us now turn to the interesting female couple Christina and Nicole. Nicole appears to be a woman of very few words. Her delivery is clipped, even though she runs words together in a colloquial and somewhat lazy way. Civility is not her strongest point; she is barely polite to anyone. Her manner is tough, and she moves quickly and gets on with things.[12] Christina, for her part, seems much slower, her Latin American inflection slowing down her delivery, making it softer and – we feel – more lengthy and deliberate than Nicole's. Interestingly, however, Nicole speaks only half as often as Christina, yet she delivers just as many words! A study of the script shows that Nicole speaks 186 times to Christina's 370 and that Nicole utters 2,115 words in those utterances and Christina 2,194. By averaging out these figures, Christina speaks more often and yet, on each occasion, says less than her partner (Christina's delivery works out at just under six words per utterance; Nicole's just over 11). Yet it is noteworthy that both become more voluble after the 'murder', with an identical increase, respectively, in terms of ratio of 2:3. More to say to each other, it transpires; more persuading, more fighting as well. However, several nuances need to be made here. From what we are saying so far it would appear that Nicole is the more dominant, with her verbal rapid-fire. Yet this is not quite the case. A graph plotting the moments (12 in all) when they do have extended exchanges (over 30 words) shows that, after their early chat in part one, sitting by the swimming pool (when Nicole dominates), it is consistently Christina who is the lengthier in each case. Just to take one example: in part four, when Nicole is starting to break down and declares that she feels she is in a madhouse (59 words), Christina retorts with almost 50% more words (81), accusing Nicole of having dragged her into this crazy story of murder. So, on the verbal level at least, Christina is not as feeble as she first appears. Clearly, power relations are not stable here at all.

As we know, the two women have entered into a complicitous relationship against Michel. A complicity which, to the viewer, is utterly convincing since we do not know, until the very end of the film, that Michel and Nicole have been plotting to cause Christina's eventual heart attack. In other words, we are led to believe that what we are seeing is the truth, the duplicity being revealed only at the last minute. During this period of seeing what we believe to be the truth, we witness the close friendship between the two women. Indeed, as M. Drain remarks, although they should be rivals, in fact they are close allies – which he finds abnormal. This closeness is clearly signalled by the number of two-shots of the women together (82 in all) as opposed to those of Michel and Nicole, who are almost never in a two-shot (there are only six), or, again, those of Michel with his wife (15). This female-to-female relationship, then, has greater visual importance than any of the others. Even the three-shots are few and far between, which is unusual given that that there is a triangular relationship between, these three main characters (there are only 11 three-shots). Thus, the actual framing of the characters lulls us into this belief that the relationship between Nicole and Christina is a close, primary and even intimate one. Indeed, there are two specific moments when this is visually hinted at. First, when at Niort, there is a shot of them in bed together just after they have 'murdered' Michel. Later, once back at the school, the two women are framed in a bedroom window in their night-clothes, in the background a double bed, untidily unmade as if slept in. In this latter shot, Nicole is wearing dark pyjamas and Christina white ones. Nicole stands, as if protectively, behind Christina. They stand framed like any couple might. But this light/dark motif that runs throughout warns us that not all is unambiguous. Nicole wears dark, severe utilitarian-styled dresses with straight skirts firmly belted at the waist, while Christina wears light coloured patterns with full skirts (which hint at her Latin American origins).[13] The only reversal in colouring is with the hair: Nicole's hair is blonde and cropped short, whereas Christina's is long and dark. However, this reversal in colour does nothing to undo the image of Christina's exotic foreignness and femininity, as opposed to Nicole's more severe, 'masculinised' appearance. Thus, Christina comes over as the exotic fragile female and Nicole as a strong-willed, modern woman. Unlike Christina, who has given over her economic rights to Michel through marriage, Nicole is economically independent. Not only does she have a paid job, she is also a property owner. She is purposeful and no-nonsense,

Penny-pinching Nicole at the petrol pump

hard-nosed and penny-pinching – a flaw that will be her undoing (see picture on page 49). Nicole smokes her cigarette in a 'masculine' manner, pulling the butt from her mouth with her thumb and forefingers and stamping it out on the ground with considerable force. She is quite 'masculinised', therefore, in relation to Christina. Furthermore, she teaches sciences, 'hard' male-identified subjects, as opposed to Chistina's softer subjects (English and geometry). As the science teacher, it is Nicole who obtains the sleeping draught and knows the right amount to put into the whisky bottle, which only then will Christina be allowed to pour and serve to Michel. The roles are clearly defined here, and as far as we know it is Nicole who devised the crime.

However, not all is 'masculine' in Nicole. Her black high heels and slimline dresses are, of course, markers within the thriller codes and conventions of her femme fatale status. Iconically speaking, then, she represents here the traditional femme fatale of the film noir, with her clothing marking her as the safely contained phallic woman. However, this apparent investment in noir iconography stops dead in its tracks at this juncture with regard to Nicole's clothing. Other things intrude to stop it short. The carpet slippers she wears while carrying out the murder and, again, at the end of the film, when she is finally apprehended for her crime, do enormous damage to her status as a sexy femme fatale. How can this home-body in any way be associated with the glamour of the phallic woman of the film noir genre? Her gestures lose their extraordinariness, their excess. But there is more in terms of this undoing. For, when she is supposedly at her most ritualistically phallic moment (killing the male), her dress code stresses her ordinariness. She is in carpet slippers (like her elderly tenant upstairs) and her dress is unbelted so that it hangs, totally unrevealing of any contours, like a shapeless housecoat. That is one way in which the iconographic coding is in conflict. But there are others. The casually worn cardigan over the shoulders suggests a sporty persona (ready for tennis) not associated with the languorous femme fatale. And even that iconography (of sportswoman) is destabilised by the fact that Nicole knits (presumably for herself – a new white cardigan perhaps?), although her needles do flash with considerable vigour, pointing to her prickly nature. Curiously, as if to give weight to this conflictual or fragmented characterisation, it is noteworthy that she is not (as she would have been in a traditional film noir) the object of Michel's investigatory gaze. She is not, therefore, the enigma that has to be unravelled – which, as a femme fatale, she most assuredly would be. Indeed, as already discussed, this probing of the enigma itself gets fragmented. In the first instance there is a reversal of this film noir trope and it is Michel who, once he has been 'murdered', becomes the enigmatically vanished body that is the constant object of the two females' searching gaze – he becomes the '*Laura*' figure. And, in the second instance, it is the rather grubby, unkempt and sleazy-looking retired policeman turned private eye, Inspector Fichet (Charles Vanel), who probes and investigates Christina, and *not* Nicole (again with the effect of deflating her femme fatale role), to get at the truth and resolve the mystery. Finally, in this series of role reversals, where the two men are concerned, to Michel's rather feminised role (as the enigmatic, evanescent body) corresponds Fichet's own lack of sexualised masculinity (even though, of course, his persistence finally pays dividends). All in all, one could argue that this is the film noir to end all films noirs.

To return to Signoret's role as Nicole: when she walks, with her grand strides, she comes over as sexually powerful – predatory, even. But here, again, there is something incomplete. As if she is lacking a target. There is no hint of passion between her and Michel (in a sense, there cannot be, or else the twist in the tale of the narrative would be given away). Thus, this power seemingly has to find another outlet, and this it does in the form of her relationship with Christina. Nicole takes charge of and has control over the other woman – much as she does in the original novel. As such she occupies a masculine space, which, in this instance, transforms their relationship into a simulacrum of the heterosexual couple. This is confirmed in a number of ways. First, on several occasions Nicole holds Christina from behind in a proprietal way that is similar to the way Michel grabs hold of his wife (pinning her arms to her side). Second, she has arguments with Christina that are more like a couple's tiffs than straightforward disagreements between friends or colleagues. For example, in one sequence the two women are sitting side by side marking the boys' homework, trying to 'behave normally'. But Christina keeps fretting about the crime. Nicole's silent seething at her partner's feeble weakness eventually reaches breaking point and she begins to make all sorts of brutal gestures, including violently throwing a pencil rubber over at her. And right at the end of the film Nicole, much as if she were part of a couple, comes to the tearful conclusion that 'it will be better if we separate'.

In his review of this film, Derek Prowse speaks of Signoret as 'big and dominating' and Vera Clouzot as 'small and harassed'.[14] Within these sets of contrasts, Nicole looms as the dark shadow to Christina's virginal translucence. Theirs is not quite a 'butch-femme' relationship, however, even though it appears to come close. As we shall see, it meets with several twists that challenge this stereotype. Nicole orders Christina about magisterially but also comforts her when she is abused by Michel. But, as with all the other embodiments mentioned above, the dramatic tension stops there and things start to contradict themselves and fragment as the film tries to reassert its heterosexual bias. In a sense, the fact of heterosexualising the narrative gets in the way of the plot having conviction, denaturalises it, forces it to a series of grinding halts. Several critics of the time make the point that the plot is empty, absurd.[15] That is far too harsh. Even though they do have a point that something does not quite gel (for the reasons I have suggested), the film is nonetheless full of suspense and minute observations, which together make it compelling to watch. And what makes it compelling to watch in particular are the moments when the complicity of the two women is forefronted. We get a grip on a narrative line that seems to be taking us somewhere – and that 'somewhere' is into their relationship – but, as soon as we move away, things become dislocated, contradictory even. Thus, the lesbian intertext is always co-present clashing with the re-inscription of the heterosexual one. Interestingly, even within the now straight version of the story, we are not totally without sympathy for these two women. For example, the murder scene where they drug and eventually drown Michel in the bathtub is a masterful piece of horror. And yet we believe we understand their motivation, given how much they have suffered at the sadistic hand of this man of whom they are now (apparently) disposing themselves.

Just as this film fluctuates uneasily between text and intertext (as described above), so too the narrative fluctuates between two contradictory types of relationships. First, there is the intense same-sex relationship between Nicole and Christina. Second, there is the doubly dosed sado-masochistic one between Michel and his wife, on the one hand, and Michel and Nicole on the other. In the novel there is no real match to this. We hardly meet up with the lesbian couple. Only at the end, once the twist in the plot is revealed, do we realise what their true relationship was, so nothing is developed there. Nor do we get much sense of the husband-and-wife relationship. The only point of comparison between the two texts, then, is the rather nasty dynamic between the doctor (Lucienne) and her supposed lover (the husband), which is the relationship that dominates the novel's narrative. Meantime, Clouzot has filled his own film text with an extraordinary set of relational mirrorings and complexities that make his narrative far denser and in excess of the original. I would argue that there are three reasons for this textual density. First, this greater density comes down to the complexity of Nicole and Christina's relationship. It can, as I have already explained, be seen as a simulacrum of the heterosexual relationship (so a first inverted mirroring of sorts). However, it can equally be seen for what it is (albeit the filmic text tries to hide it away), namely a lesbian relationship. It can also be seen as a mother-daughter relationship. Nicole takes care of Christina; she speaks to her at times as a mother would to a daughter. Patiently and meticulously she explains why the murder must be carried out and why it must be carried out in a particular way. She is protective of her sexual immaturity. She soothes her when Michel is cruel to her (and so on). Already, we are looking at three types of ambiguity here, unfixing the social order of things. Nothing remains in place. Thus, it should not surprise us there is also a power shift within this same-sex relationship. Christina, who at first seems so submissive to Nicole's dominant ways, takes the upper hand once they fail to discover the body in the swimming pool. Christina, collapses at first but then recovers her lost sang-froid and becomes more forceful. After this moment, it is Nicole who apparently begins to be full of fear (describing the whole thing as madness) and Christina who begins to criticise Nicole's plan, even to the point of trying to lay all the responsibility at Nicole's feet – something she later backs away from as her Catholicism gets the better of her. When Michel's suit turns up, she manages, just like the flawed noir heroes before her, to find the strength from somewhere to take on board the enigma that has to be solved. So, briefly, she occupies the masculine space of investigator.

Nicole, meantime, appears to become less than useless, and when the hotel visit fails to top Christina (i.e. kill her off) she has to resort to desperate means to prevent Christina from both confessing her crime in church and to the police – which she is close to doing. Fortuitously, a body is discovered in the Seine. But, by capitalising on that piece of seeming good fortune and encouraging Christina to follow it up, Nicole makes her fatal mistake (as all femmes fatales must!). Thanks to this hopeless gesture on Nicole and Christina's part, the private detective gets involved in the story. Unbeknown to us, the tables have turned on the real plot. Although Fichet now takes charge of resolving the enigma surrounding Michel, Christina remains the more powerful of the two women (as far as we can determine). She dismisses Nicole from her sight, and as the private detective becomes increasingly nosy with his questions it is she who fields them with intelligence, while Nicole becomes more and more anxious. Of course, at the end of the film we come to understand why Nicole reacts so badly to the detective's intrusive questions (because he might blow apart the scheme to cause Christina's death). But until then it looks as if there is a role reversal and Christina has taken command both of the situation and Nicole.

Thus, a first reason for this textual density comes down to the intensity of this same-sex relationship, where, on the one hand, power relations shift and, on the other, sexual positionings as well as sexuality itself shift from straight to queer; and, as we have seen, Michel's positioning is equally far from stable. A second reason comes down to the fact that the film adaptation has a political intertext that is not at all present within the original novel (first printed in 1952). And it is here that we need to take a closer look at this period of the 1950s and what was going on in contemporary France. In her study of this period, Kristin Ross argues that the emphasis in France on the modernisation and cleansing of cities and households during the post-war period, and more especially the 1950s, is far more complex than a mere drive to appear a modern European society.[16] Ross explains how France underwent a massive desire to be clean, starting, as we have seen, with the work of the Cleansing Committees (*Comités d'épuration*) in the immediate aftermath of the war. This cleansing went further than these judicial committees. It included social hygiene, in the form of closing down brothels (the *loi Marthe Richard*, 1947). As we know, Clouzot was himself subject to a fairly draconian sentence by the Cleansing Committees, yet repeatedly in his films he shows just how murky and unclean French society is as a whole – with perhaps an extra emphasis on the petite bourgeoisie, of which most of the characters in *Les Diaboliques* are exemplary. So, this film speaks to this moment of France's history, suggesting that such cleansing is no simple affair.

In this context, this film can also be read as redolent with the immeasurable guilt that is the legacy of the Occupation.[17] Guilt is everywhere, pervasive and yet paradoxically ungraspable (much like Michel's disappearing body). This guilt takes the projected form of cruelty through a criss-crossing of sadomasochistic relationships that shift and mirror each other, leaving us unclear as to who, if anyone, is the victim – in fact, all the adults are monstrous. Suspicion is rife and no one, not even Christina, is a true innocent (as she herself recognises). This reading of the film, within the context of the contemporary, certainly holds true and provides some of the clues to this textual density.

But it was not just the immediate, unclean past that was being expunged in France. By the mid-1950s the drive for cleanliness and modernisation within the nation (especially in the form of electronic gadgets entering the home) masked another dirtiness, this time the dirtiness of the Algerian war – the so-called '*sale guerre*/dirty war'. This dirty war was one of the rape and torture of the Algerian community by the French army, one of guerrilla tactics on both sides with vicious bomb attacks on civilians. The torture itself was often of a type that left 'no traces', and so was called 'clean torture'. In this clean torture the French army employed electricity attached to genitals and used water-filled bathtubs to submerge prisoners and force them to confess. Meantime, back in France, in the home, the stress was continuously on the need for the French woman to be clean, to have clean children and to run a clean home (advertisement after advertisement insists upon this, with shiny new electronic homes). Ross interprets this stress on cleanliness as follows:

> In the roughly ten-year period of the mid-1950s to the mid-1960s – the decade that saw both the end of the empire and the surge in French consumption and modernization – the colonies are in some sense 'replaced', and the effort that once went into maintaining and disciplining a colonial people and situation becomes instead concentrated on a particular 'level' of metropolitan existence: everyday life. And women of course [...] are the everyday: its managers, its embodiment. The transfer of a colonial political economy to a domestic one involved a new emphasis on controlling *domesticity*, a new concentration on the political economy of the household. An efficient, well-run harmonious home is a national asset: the quality of the domestic environment has a major influence on the physique and health of the nation. A chain of equivalences is at work here; the prevailing logic runs something like this: if woman is clean, the family is clean, the nation is clean.[18]

Due to the stringencies of political censorship, after 1954, reference to this Algerian war could not be made in film, nor on TV or radio. Films alluding to it were banned. The period was one of the severest in censorship ever.

Clouzot is on record as having wanted to make a couple of films about France's colonial situation, one on the Algerian crisis and the other on the war in Indochina. But in both instances the projects were officially blocked. This is why, in an interview in 1953, he categorically states the following:

> Twice I tried. [...] The first...was in equatorial France. The French government basically refused to let me go ahead, or more precisely demanded so many changes that the scenario no longer made sense. The second subject that I was passionate about was the war in Indochina. This time the veto was absolute. Why? Because my take on the events in Africa and Asia did not tow the official line...I am not making a personal plea here. [...] However we must be clear: the censorship which exists in France today is tremendously dangerous for all of us because it is stealthy and virtually clandestine.[19]

Later on in this interview, Clouzot goes on to talk about the arbitrary nature of this censorship, which does not attack writers but does not hesitate to assail filmmakers. Clearly, here he is referring to the hardship inflicted upon him after the Occupation as much as to the frustration of having his two projects blocked. It was immediately following the blocking of his film on Indochina that he decided to adapt a thriller and discovered Boileau and Narcejac's novel. So, this adaptation does speak back to this censorship,

Moinet watches (unseen) the two women in the science lab

however subtly. The film was released in 1955, a year after the Algerian war was in the public domain, and it is clear that there are indirect references to it, particularly the use of 'clean torture'. The primary example is that of the two women's drowning of Michel in the bathtub. It is graphically represented on screen, with Nicole forcing, pushing him down under the water and holding him there to drown. She even resorts to placing a bronze statue (of a lion!) on his chest to ensure he will remain submerged. In so doing, Nicole embodies more than just the scheming murderer or femme fatale of the film noir – she becomes the military leader who sanctions the torture. Moreover, Christina, although a mere subaltern, nonetheless colludes with the murder. She becomes her partner in crime by weakly following her orders. There are, then, two, related, readings we can make of this scene. Clearly, in conducting this dirty murder, albeit through a clean torture, Nicole completely subverts the sanctioned myth of woman as clean, as the harbinger of the new modern French woman (that is, being in her home, making babies and keeping everyone and everything clean). Secondly, a subtextual reading allows us to see how, even though censorship proscribed talking truthfully about the past (the complicities and connivances of the Occupation) or the present (the torturing going on in Algeria), such a *mise en scène* can now (with hindsight) be read as a cleverly disguised counter-image to the monumental self-deception behind the post-war mythology of heroism (created via the overemphasis on the Resistance) and the triumphant rebirth into a morally pure modernity at the expense of a dirty hidden war in the colonies (in the form of the privatisation of the industrial sphere – that is, bringing the clean technological tools into the home). By making Nicole a metaphor, in this instance, for an unclean France (echoed by the dirtiness of the school and the very shabby house in Niort) we get yet another explanation as to why she occupies the least feminised of the positions in relation to the camera. This time it is not a question of not being the femme fatale. No; this time she has stepped out of the genre and become a political statement. In being dirty (and mean) she effectively counters the official ideal of a clean and abundant French womanhood, and therefore nationhood.

It is also worth pausing for a moment on Clouzot's two words (in the above quote) 'stealthy' and 'clandestine', because this brings me to my third and final reason for the density of this film text. These two terms bring in their wake the concept of the hidden and of observing unseen. The text is dense because we cannot see properly (we recall Soudieu's words '*soupe au chocolat*/chocolate soup'). Truths are hidden. Beginning with Nicole's dismissal from her former school in Niort; we never know why, any more than do M. Drain or Christina, who both mention this dismissal. Nor do M. and Mme Herboux mention it – even though they were schoolteachers in Niort, so surely, in such a small gossipy town, would have been privy to this information. Why does it suit them not to mention it when M. Herboux, for one, gets so angry at Nicole drawing the bath? He is pretty rude about her and yet does not raise this issue in his invective. Instead, we get fairly servile behaviour, as if appearances are what matter. This becomes transparently clear when Mme Herboux is most impressed by Mme Delassalle (Christina) when Nicole introduces them to each other. Impressed, doubtless, not just because she is the headmistress of the school but because it is clearly a private one, and one that she owns ('directrice' also means 'owner' in this context). So, this information shrouds the reality, just as the school itself acts as a hiding place for Nicole and the two other mediocre examples of education, M. Drain and M. Raymond, who both hold very lowly jobs. Yet even their position as *pions* does not let us move away from the idea of stealth. *Pion* (meaning 'pawn') is a familiar and somewhat derogatory term for a junior schoolteacher who has responsibility only for overseeing the pupils' homework and class preparation. Basically, s/he watches over them to make sure they work and to maintain order – a surveillance post, then. So *pion* has, by extension, come to mean 'snitch'; if someone is accused of being a *pion,* s/he is behaving like a sneak. So, these two men watch with stealth as Nicole and Christina go about their business. M. Drain comments on the unhealthiness of their relationship. The schoolboys, imitating the bad example of their elders, also observe this relationship and find it unhealthy – albeit in a different way. According to Moinet, who watches them unseen, they are secret drinkers (see picture on page 56).

In among this clandestinity and stealth we are dealing with unruly bodies. The two women, certainly in terms of the queerness of their relationship, but also on an individual level (Christina going against every principle of her faith and Nicole lying every step of the way), are prime candidates. They are unruly in other ways too. Nicole's failure to adhere to a prototype, as femme fatale, makes her unruly. Her physical and verbal aggressiveness keeps her detached from normative codes of femininity and she remains therefore somewhat asexual. Christina is determined to seek out that lost body. Her desperate refusal to accept things at face value and thereby comply easily with the role of intended victim makes her an unruly body. She has to know. And in traditional film noir narrative a woman who has to know not only is a dangerous woman, she has to be punished – as will be the case for Christina. As her 'reward' for finding Michel she gets to die; as Michel rises out of the bathtub, more flesh than spectre, her terror is complete. How ironic that when she believed she had killed him, her one regret, she declared, was that he would never know it was she 'whodunnit'.

Michel's body is the most unruly of all. It will not stay put. Moreover, in its feminisation it challenges gender boundaries – in the same way that Nicole's does, but in reverse. It also breaks other, more ethical codes. In his cynical cruelty he voices the unspeakable to his wife, namely that she should die. Surely the lowest of the low.

But so too are M. Raymond and M. Drain unruly bodies. The former proudly announces to Nicole that he is looking forward to spending his holiday in a nudist colony – to rid himself of his toxins! So, at least he knows he has something to clean out. The way in which he delivers this unwelcome bit of news is almost, though not quite, like having a dirty little secret that he feels he just must impart, probably for shock value. Nicole remains unimpressed even though there is something singularly unpleasant about the piece of information she has just received. The suggestion, let alone the reality, of him vaunting his naked body is deeply unpleasant, since he already looks so unappetising fully clothed. M. Drain, no less unpleasant, swings in entirely the opposite direction. As Nicole acerbically remarks, he has spent too long with the Jesuits – the strictest form of Catholicism. So, while he busily reassures himself of his moral rectitude with his snide little grins and believes unfalteringly that he occupies the high moral ground, almost everything he utters makes him sound like a hypocritical sour prune. Physically, Pierre Larquey as M. Drain manages a wonderful performance here with his body. By contorting it into a sanctimonious smugness at the same time as making it appear totally desiccated, he embodies brilliantly this failed teacher's contempt for others and yet simultaneously reveals how brittle he is within.

Finally, Inspector Fichet. Because, for different reasons, neither Christina nor Nicole were able to keep their sang-froid and stick to the plan (indeed, to two different plans, as it also transpires), Fichet gets drawn into the story. Nicole had not counted on Christina having a crisis of conscience, which means she has to play a card she had never intended to play. The card of reality: a real body found in the Seine. This seeming bit of serendipity, however, works against the two of them. It brings into play the last of the unruly bodies: Fichet. It is noteworthy that he was always already poised had he been called upon to investigate (any incident), since he lurks with intent at the morgue. Unable to accept that he is officially in retirement, he carries on his trade irrespective of his present lack of real status. He even manages to hold onto his warrant card, surely an indication of his ability and willingness to bend rules. As his name implies, Fichet *s'en fiche* – literally, he could care less. He is no respecter of Christina or Nicole's reticence and runs roughshod over their protestations. As his name also implies, *fichier* (meaning card index box), he notes everything down; nothing escapes his attention, such as Michel's Prince of Wales suit hanging up behind the door (had he not been so meticulous he might not have spotted it). This grubby ex-representative of the law is a peculiar agent of order, since neither of the women (for opposite reasons) want him there. And, just as surely as he solves the mystery for Christina, so too he causes the two schemers to accelerate their plans to kill her. If only he had told Christina exactly what he had found out, she might not have been led on her last morbid dance towards death. She would no longer have had the curiosity to follow shadows down corridors, open doors on clacking typewriters, and finally collapse at the feet of her not dead husband.

So, to answer the title of this section, what sort of film is this? The answer has to be a transgressive and transcendent film noir. There is fragmentation and excess, both of which are played out through the narrative and the body, and both of which function to challenge the constructed order of things, social restrictions, established laws and hierarchies as they relate to notions of censorship and sexuality. This makes it a far less conservative or classical narrative film than it might at first appear. With regard to this transgressive nature of the film, it is true that Christina does die in the end and that the two conspirators do get found out (unlike in the novel, where we are left to believe that, having got away with the crime, maybe Lucienne will now get rid of her rather sickly lover, Mireille). So order of a sort is re-established in the concluding moments of the film (by a very scruffy and unphallic patriarch, Fichet), but not before a great deal of social disruption has taken place in which gender norms and political censorship are challenged. Sexual and political boundaries within this film have been stretched (transgressed even) beyond the historical and ideological order in which it was produced (the mid-1950s) – a time of severe censorship, a desire to control the female body and profound homophobia. So, it was an extraordinary film for its time. Despite its unease as to its nature (as straight or queer), this was a very high-scoring film, with an audience of 3.7 million. People go to see thrillers to be frightened. They also go because it is the chance to see a representation of the unrepresentable. The attraction lies in the challenge to the architectonics of social order – the carnivalesque disruption of knowable boundaries. And it is surely this that makes this film still hold such fascination for audiences today.

Notes

1   Krutnik, Frank (1991), p. 17.
2   Vincendeau, Ginette, unpublished chapter on 'French film noir in the classical era', p. 15. I am indebted to the author for letting me have an advance copy of this chapter for reference.
3   Krutnik (1991), p. 45.
4   Ibid., p. xiv.
5   Ibid. p. 63.
6   Vincendeau, Ginette, 'French film noir in the classical era', p. 16.
7   Ibid., p. 6.
8   Ibid., p. 10.
9   Ibid., p. 10.
10   Ibid., p. 17.
11   There is a sketch of the type of dress Signoret wears in *Les Diaboliques* in the French Communist Party's women's weekly *Heures Claires des Femmes Françaises*, 4 November 1954, p. 14. Called a sort of 'passe-partout', its qualities are extolled by the weekly since it is functional, smart and inexpensive to purchase.
12   Nicole will always go for the shortest sentence possible. For example, she says: 'Vous dérangez pas/Don't bother yourself', not: 'Ne vous dérangez pas/Please don't bother yourself.' She is extremely uncivil; she introduces Mme Herboux to Christina by way of shorthand. 'Mme Herboux, agrégée de grammaire; Mme Delassalle, directrice de l'école où je fonctionne/Mme Herboux BA in grammar; Mme Delassalle, headmistress where I work.'
13   In 1954 *Heures Claires des Femmes Françaises* spoke very favourably of the utilitarian nature of this day dress, that was in vogue during that year; 4 November 1954, p. 14.
14   Prowse, Derek, review of *Les Diaboliques*, *Sight and Sound* 25 (3), 1955/1956, p. 149.

15 See, for example, Prowse's review in *Sight and Sound*, *Variety*'s review (23 February 1956, no page) and Pierre Theberge's review, 'Chéri fais-moi peur/ Darling frighten me', in *Objectif* 2 (17), 1962, pp. 37–38.

16 Ross, Kristin (1995), pp. 80–92.

17 See Herpe, Noël, in *Positif*, January 1996, pp. 103–105.

18 Ross (1995), pp.77–78.

19 Clouzot in an interview with *L'Express*, 5 December 1953, quoted in Pilard (1969), pp. 111–112.

4   Sequence analysis

In this chapter we focus on three sequences. These analyses will serve to uncover in more detail the difference in characterisation between the three main protagonists (Nicole, Christina and Michel), observe more finely the dynamics between them, comment upon their performances as actors and, finally, examine more closely how camera work and *mise en scène* function in each instance to enhance performance, underline the atmosphere or convey a specific sense of space.

To begin with, we shall look at what could loosely be termed the establishing sequence of part one; then the 'murder' sequence in Nicole's apartment in Niort; lastly the terrorising of Christina until her death.

Setting the scene (4m. 30s.)

In part one we are introduced to the three main protagonists within and via the school environment. We meet them one by one, each carrying out their duties as providers. Michel is the one we meet first, when he returns from the market with food for the school. As the provider we very quickly learn that he is an extremely poor one (he brings home 'rotten salads', and as we find out later he is perfectly happy to serve up rotten fish, to his staff and pupils alike). But now it is break time and we enter the school, where we meet up with Nicole, and a little later Christina, as they leave their classrooms and take their break. It is the introduction of these two central female characters and their subsequent meeting with Michel in the science lab that

I want to discuss. As we shall see, we receive a great deal of information in the four minutes and 30 seconds of this sequence.

We get the measure of Nicole, first, by the way in which she lets her pupils out of the classroom. She commands them to exit ('Sortez!') and they do so in orderly fashion, two by two, as she claps out a rhythm (a military 'one, two, one, two') for them to file out by, silent with their arms folded. This extreme obedience on the part of her pupils contrasts with the unruly way in which M. Drain's pupils left his classroom – as we witnessed just moments earlier – and, similarly, M. Raymond's class. Both give full evidence of having no control over their pupils whatsoever. They run down the corridor, charge down the stairs, jostle each other and trip each other up. No pupil would dare behave in such a way or cross Mademoiselle Nicole Horner. But our first visual impression of Nicole is equally striking. She comes out of her classroom door into the corridor, where the camera is currently focusing on MM. Drain and Raymond's conversation. She enters into the frame in the foreground to the right, then turns to face the camera in middle shot. We are stunned to find her wearing sunglasses. They add to the hardness of her features, but, principally, we cannot understand why she needs them on. Nor, indeed, can we see what her eyes are doing. This startling effect is compounded by the fact that it is a damp, grey day (a point Christina makes a little later when she expresses her longing for the sun) – so the glasses are clearly hiding something.

This sense of mystery continues when M. Drain twice makes sarcastic comments to Nicole, who has now joined them in the corridor. He un-interestedly asks her if she is well, since early in the morning he heard such a rumpus going on in her room (with shouting and the like). Nicole attempts to brush him off as if he were a smelly fly – accusing him of having stayed too long with the Jesuits. However, Drain gets the last word. As he leaves, he snidely comments that not everyone can get themselves dismissed from school (referring here to Nicole's previous employment, we presume). What makes this scene work so effectively – be so natural, even – is the fact that, during this whole 'bitchy' exchange (held mostly in a medium three-shot), each of the three teachers is doing something with his or her hands. While Drain attempts to put Nicole down, Raymond, to the left of the frame, gazes laconically at her as he removes a small paper bag of sweets from his right-hand pocket and begins popping them into his mouth. His dry look, continuous silence and methodical gestures of sweet-popping make him a rather unpleasant witness to Drain's attempt at Nicole's humiliation. Drain, positioned in the centre of the three, is busying himself preparing a roll-up cigarette, all the while discoursing on Nicole's dissipated early morning behaviour – a clever strategy for shrouding his words with an aura of innocence (he looks as if he is passing the time of day, but in fact he is being really nasty). Nicole, for her part, is holding a cigarette packet in her right hand. She has her back to us and is in semi-profile to the right of the frame. She has already extracted a cigarette and put it in her mouth. But she has not yet managed to light it, interrupted as she is by Drain's ironic incantation of lines, as if from a poem: 'The virtuous woman delights in contemplating dawn rising…' We can sense her annoyance at his superciliousness since she begins to tap her packet on her left hand (almost as if she is beating in rhythm to his lines, but her tapping is more indicative of her desire to take a swipe at him). At this point the camera cuts and is positioned behind Raymond, faced onto Nicole, as she delivers her sarcastic retort to Drain about the Jesuits. In other words, we get to see her face in full – composed, cool and frosty – sending her punchline back to Drain. We do not, however, have Drain in counter-shot. The triangulation has effectively skewed the sight lines and so obliges the camera to be behind Raymond to catch Nicole's face. To have taken the shot from behind Drain (her interlocutor) would have meant, technically, keeping Nicole in profile, albeit this time from the front, with the net result that the impact of her cutting words would not have been as strong. The choice to frame her full frontal makes sense because it ensures that the total impact of her stinging words is not lost (ultimately, on the audience). Finally, in this scene, the camera resumes the earlier three-shot position and Drain pushes his way (almost triumphantly, since he knows he has struck a chord) between Raymond and Nicole as he delivers, upon exiting, his last nasty line (see photograph on page 66). Nicole and Raymond watch him go. Nicole, half beaten, utters a rude and vulgar parting shot: 'Le chameau/Jerk.'

Drain links us to the next set of shots, which introduce Christina to us. He walks up to her as her class begins to disperse. Interestingly, none of her pupils seems to be in any hurry to leave. They are an assorted bunch of young boys, including a black pupil and a Venezuelan, and they hang around as if there were no reason to rush off. It is almost as if they find comfort in her own otherness as a Latin American – as if she embodies family, motherhood/land. One of them, Josélito, is so smitten with Christina that he offers her a gift, a Spanish fan from Venezuela. And it is through this object that we begin to learn something about her, where she comes from, how much she loves the sun of her homeland (Venezuela). She appears sweet and gentle, she uses terms of endearment to thank Josélito: 'Thank you, sweetie.' Clearly, M. Drain is also attracted to her nice nature, and elects to walk with her a while, engaging in conversation with her and listening. These soft interchanges between her and her pupils and Drain contrast vividly with what has just passed (noisy boisterous schoolboys, sharp and inflexible schoolmistress, snide exchanges). Also, as if to demarcate her persona strongly from Nicole's, Christina is wearing a summer dress with lots of flounce about it. It is decidedly feminine in its look, against the no-nonsense, straight pencil-line dress Nicole wears. The actual fabric of her dress is a lively gingham, in contrast to Nicole's black, suggesting a youthful, schoolgirly disposition. It is full of design features: a low-square cut neck, and a full, gently pleated A-line skirt, suggesting many petticoats underneath to give it bulk (hinting at an exotic sexuality beneath). Her skirt sways with the body's movement, Nicole's decidedly does not (in fact, the pencil-line cut restricts her leg movements). Christina carries a shawl, again a symbol of her exotic Latin American provenance, whereas Nicole wears, over her strong shoulders, a perfectly neat

M. Drain exits triumphant

white cardigan with classical lines. Rigid neatness and utility versus verve and a touch of exotica; thus can be summed up the meaning of our two female protagonists' sartorial appearance. But Christina's clothing (like her words to Drain and her gesture of fanning herself with her new gift) also serves to confirm her desire to be elsewhere – back in Venezuela. These clothes are far from practical in a cold and damp environment. There are other clues to Christina: her dark hair is neatly parted and distributed into two very tidy plaits, which are joined at the bottom with a velvet bow. The hairstyle suggests less a sultry, sexual Latin American (which loose long hair swept up with a Spanish comb most definitely would have done) than an obedient schoolgirl – and we have already noted that the gingham print of her dress points to a schoolgirlishness. And this is the point at which Christina's iconography starts to look less stable than Nicole's. Her dress code now becomes more that of an immature young woman than a woman in her mid-30s (which is her real age). And, indeed, as the narrative progresses through the first half of the film, Nicole and Michel noticeably treat her more like a child than a grown adult.

Christina's walk with Drain brings her back to where Nicole was last seen. In a single medium shot, Nicole looks up from her newspaper to observe Christina, Josélito and Drain approaching. They do not see her. As Christina shoos Josélito away, she turns around in single medium shot to find Nicole still peering at her.[1] Christina realises immediately that the presence of the sunglasses means something is wrong. As soon as she sees the black eye she knows what has happened: 'Miguel?' she states rhetorically. We note that they 'tutoie' each other (the familiar form in French), suggesting some kind of intimacy; they are friends, perhaps. But what is interesting in this short scene is what the camera work tells us about them. The scene, all in medium shot, opens with a series of single shots: one on each woman (Christina, then Nicole), after which Christina moves into frame with Nicole and it becomes a two-shot; they exchange a few words. Nicole then moves out of frame, leaving Christina in single-shot; they are still talking. Cut to Nicole, who is looking in a large mirror at her bruised eye and commenting on Michel (wondering how Christina put up with him so long). Cut back to Christina, who defends her husband ('He wasn't always like that'); cut to Nicole, who says something snide about Michel and Christina ('He stuck with you for the money'), and once again it is Christina who enters the frame, this time going up close to Nicole and taking hold gently of her arms, more or less saying let's not quarrel ('Life is hard enough'). We then cut away to M. Drain and M. Raymond, who have been watching all this, and Drain exclaims that he finds the intimacy between the two women extraordinary; how can the legitimate wife be drying the tears of the mistress? Cut back to the two women leaving the hallway, in long shot. Christina puts on her shawl, Nicole helps her adjust it around the shoulders, holds onto her arms and gently ushers her upstairs, where she has something she wants to show her. There is a balance in the shooting of this scene. First, Christina enters twice into an intimate spatial relationship with Nicole (she comes into Nicole's frame, the first time to express concern, the second to hold her), and then, later, Nicole reciprocates that intimacy as they leave the scene. That scene is also read for us by Drain. As far as the audience is concerned we have witnessed (and had it verbally confirmed by Drain) that what we are seeing is both extraordinary but true: the two women do comfort each other. There is a tenderness between the two, which is slowly constructed in these early scenes (as in the refectory scene a bit later, when Nicole stands up against Michel for Christina and goes over to comfort her). A slow construction, which makes the tender intimacy utterly believable, but which, of course, is a total smokescreen (as we find out eventually).

Before drawing any final conclusions on the above, let us now consider the entry of Michel into the frame in the following sequence. He comes across the two women for the first time when he spots them in a science lab. Once again, it is a third party that links this scene to the former one, this time in the form of the pupil Moinet. He is skipping along the corridor when he notices that Nicole and Christina are in the lab and that Nicole is showing Christina a bottle, the contents of which she makes her smell. We cannot hear what they are saying since the point of view is Moinet's (outside the lab, peering in). We cut into the lab, looking out at Moinet's face pressed against the pane of glass. At no point are the two women aware they are being watched. We then hear footsteps in the corridor. Moinet hears them and scuttles away. The camera is still inside the lab looking out towards the glass-paned door. The two women have heard nothing. Michel comes into frame holding his cigarette holder in his left hand. He observes the two women momentarily before bursting in on them. Cut to Nicole, who quickly hides the bottle in her pocket. Cut to Michel. He closes the door. Cut back to Nicole, who swiftly closes the display cabinet door from which she had taken the bottle. Cut to Michel as he advances on them and joins up with them in a three-shot. As he enters the lab he is harsh, brutal. He shouts at them, asking what they are doing there as if they are two naughty schoolchildren. Indeed, when Christina replies: 'Nothing' he mimics her nastily, saying they are just like kids. This belittling them comes full circle at the end of the sequence, when he chucks them out of the lab, sending them off to the playground shouting: 'Go out and play, you two!' The tone has changed from the previous sequence; the mood has become aggressive as Michel attacks the two women verbally and physically. First, he assaults Christina and brutally forces a kiss on her. He then wipes his mouth with his handkerchief as if it were he who had had the nasty experience (as if he had been smeared with her filth). Later, at the end of the sequence, he grabs hold of Nicole and throws her towards the door with such force she almost falls over.

Michel is snappily dressed, suggesting a man who likes fine clothes. But what really reveals his menacing nature is the subtle use he makes of his cigarette holder (and here the actor Paul Meurisse is truly masterful). He gestures around with it slowly in a studied and measured way, holding it delicately as if it were a sharp instrument; at times he twists it very slowly between his thumb and forefinger as if thinking sinister thoughts – it acts, then, as a metaphorical tool of torture. One imagines Michel twisting the knife into someone in this way or smoothly crushing their body with his hands (as he does Christina on two occasions, in this sequence when he kisses her and later at the end of the refectory sequence). Having battered away at the two women throughout this scene he then – having got rid of them – finally places the cigarette holder in his mouth, his face icily impassive. The cruel master dominates.

This is the sequence in which we get to learn about the dynamics of the triangular relationship, so, unsurprisingly, just over half of all the three-shots occur here (six out of the 11). What we learn is how predatory Michel is; he walks in violently on the two women and asserts his place in the threesome (the first three-shot). We see how he can break up the triangle by removing one woman from it to assault her – he goes after Christina as she tries to avoid him kissing her, clinching her in a two-shot (he so overpowers her we see only his back and her protesting hands). We also witness how verbally cruel and abusive he can be, primarily towards his wife, whom he

calls a 'little ruin'. But the dynamics of the triangle are quite revealing and
do not just show Michel as the all-powerful and masterful phallic male. There
is some subtlety going on, and there are three particular moments worth
pointing out. First of all, Nicole refuses to kiss Michel on demand, showing
that she is not one to be dominated, can withhold favours as a punishment
for the black eye. Second, once Michel has finished kissing Christina (a cruel
act of substitution and displacement of aggression), he questions why she is
not in the playground monitoring, since that is where she is supposed to be.
At that precise moment Nicole enters back into the frame, reconstituting
the triangle, and says that it is she who gave Christina a dispensation. In so
doing, of course, she has undermined Michel's authority – thus, incidentally,
doubling the effect of the earlier rejection of his phallic power. Furthermore,
by coming back into the frame, Nicole asserts her ability to create the triangle
as much as Michel. Normatively within Freudian and Lacanian psychoanalysis
it is the patriarch who enters into the frame to assert the law of the father.
However, here it is Nicole who occupies that position, thus usurping Michel's
authority on two counts (by taking his place and by granting Christina a
dispensation). This moment, then, restores Nicole as the dominant female,
able to occupy a masculine space. Small wonder he has to use such force to
disengage her from that position by literally throwing her out of the room!

Finally, on these dynamics, when Nicole comes back into the triangle she
forms a base with Michel as they begin to discuss Christina's well-being. This
moment is followed by a series of three-shots, shot in shot and counter-shot.
The first shot is from Christina's point of view, looking at Nicole and Michel;
the second from Nicole and Michel's, looking at Christina. There are three
shots from Christina's point of view, two from Nicole and Michel's. The
three shots from Christina's point of view allow us to see Nicole's reaction to
Michel's particularly nasty remark about his wife (that she is a ruin); she is
shocked and looks away – thus allowing us and Christina to believe that
she has compassion for her. This impression is compounded by Nicole's
expression of concern about Christina's health, which again gets seen from
Christina's point of view. The two other three-shots, which intercut with
these, say a great deal about the power dynamics between the three. Nicole
and Michel are at the base and Christina at the apex of the triangle, literally
pinioned in the middle between the gaze of the other two. She stands there,
almost frozen by their gaze, like a naughty child being reprimanded – in this

instance, for the unsuitable shoes she wears. We hear only Michel's voice from the base of the triangle telling her off, not Nicole's. In this exchange Michel appears to have the upper hand when he says: 'Quand on est malade il faut pas être coquette/When one is ill one mustn't be coquettish.' However, Christina's answer is quite interesting. She doesn't say: 'I am not coquettish' but: 'I am not ill.' In fact, she knows full well that she is ill, so it is her choice not to refute her love of style that is interesting. She may not have much power against Michel's bullying, and, indeed, her response could be read very much as that of a child who is caught out and yet protests her innocence, all the while hiding something. However, there is some defiance in her reply; she is not yet completely beaten down. That will occur with the second of these three-shots, when she says nothing at all and just casts her eyes down, defeated by his contemptuous remarks.

The only moment of gaiety in this opening sequence is Christina's brief expression of happiness with her present from Josélito. Here she smiles radiantly as she flutters her fan and joyously explains to M. Drain the wonders of her warm country. Vera Clouzot, at this juncture, is so utterly convincing in her simple pleasure and embodiment of naivety that we have no difficulty in identifying with her as the victim of Michel's brutality. There is nothing ambiguous about her. She exudes a child-like innocence, unlike Nicole, whom we believe (rightly, as it transpires) is pretty tough and can look after herself very well. Signoret and Clouzot are well matched in their characterisation of direct opposites. But one senses it is as well that Clouzot's character is not that complex, given, with one or two exceptions, the overall woodenness of her performance. Her inability to give much of a performance gets hidden, however, by the fact that we perceive her all along as the victim; thus we do not necessarily expect a great deal more from her. But it is also the case that Signoret's complexity as a performer does a great deal to cover Clouzot's shortcomings – the most important of which (given the tight camerawork) is her inability to make her face provide a nuanced performance. Signoret's face pouts, sulks, fumes, retorts, gets cross, becomes tender; often within a matter of seconds it can shift subtly and dramatically. Clouzot's can offer none of this. It is either expressionless or, as we shall see in the actual murder scene, limited to a shift to the opposite extreme: expressing shock through eyebrow-lifting, popping eyes and an open mouth. Meurisse for his part beautifully conveys the icy, spiteful villain that he is; his performance is, like Signoret's, nuanced, cleverly balancing irony with barely concealed menace. At this stage the most interesting character, arguably, is Signoret's, because it is the most ambiguous. Indeed, this whole sequence has served to bring out a considerable number of contradictions surrounding Nicole. She has a murky past, she is involved in a tempestuous relationship with Michel, she appears harsh and yet she is tender with Christina. Things are not quite clear where she is concerned – a fact that is signified by her wearing sunglasses, which she only occasionally removes. We cannot read her eyes. So, for example, at the end of the above sequence, when she looks back at Michel after he has thrown them out of the lab, we have no idea what her glance might be saying. Little do we realise that her inscrutability is the absolute key to the devilish scheme she and Michel have concocted to rid themselves of Christina – yet here is the very clue (in the form of the sunglasses) under our noses!

This inability to read, or understand, what is seen is a central theme running through this opening sequence – and sets the tone for the rest of the film. In all the various goings-on there are male witnesses to the women's behaviour. At different moments Drain, Moinet and Michel observe Christina and Nicole, but none of them interprets what they see correctly. Drain sees the tenderness between the two women and finds it outrageous, but for the wrong reasons. He reads it as unseemly behaviour, breaking common rules of decency and etiquette. Ironically, his words are correct; it *is* outrageous, because it is all part of Nicole's con-game – but he cannot see through it, any more than we can. It is outrageous because this impropriety is a lie, not a truth. Moinet reads things incorrectly as well. He believes the two women are secret drinkers and explains their odd friendship that way. However, as with Drain before him, he gets the principle partially right. He reads what he sees as adult misbehaviour, which it is (plotting to murder). It is just that he takes their actions at face value (as Drain did earlier) and thinks they are swigging whisky. Michel knows they are up to no good in the lab, but in the end he does not probe or seek to find out what they are really up to. He (as we later discover, deliberately) overlooks the truth, takes their 'misdemeanour' at face value and exploits the situation to his advantage by using this moment to abuse the two women instead.

Throughout this set of establishing scenes, Clouzot uses characters as links between spaces and people. This linking is not just a question of narrative economy; it also helps to establish a sense of space in a particular way. Not only does it offer us a limited view (we see only where these characters take us), it also suggests that space is somewhat confined and can be quickly traversed (an important consideration, as we shall see, when we come to the third of our sequence analyses). Corridors appear to interconnect and people are encountered, often engaged in the activity of watching. Drain and Raymond watch Nicole. Nicole watches Christina, Drain and Josélito. First Moinet, then Michel, watch Nicole and Christina. So many relays of looking make for a fairly repressive atmosphere. A tight web of observance – which is given even greater emphasis by the presence of windows, glass panes and frames within frames. And yet, paradoxically, it is also a space that can easily be penetrated without too much censorship – people go where they should not (including children, as is the case for Moinet). So, despite the fact that people are doing so much watching, it is becoming clear that they are not watching effectively, since there is no sense of control emanating from it. There is, rightfully, a sense of chaos that emerges from this inability to observe properly. Surveillance is malfunctioning. Not only are things not what they seem, structures are already in the process of breaking down. Clouzot was right when he realised he needed the boarding school as the backdrop to his thriller. Within this framework of institutional collapse, anything is possible.

'Murder' sequence – Niort (14m. 47s.)

This sequence begins with the sound of Michel's footsteps and ends with the fade on Christina and Nicole in bed – their deed accomplished. Considerable attention is given to footwear in this part of the film. Nicole's carpet slippers allow her to move around silently (note, for example, that Christina does not hear her enter the bathroom). Christina wears the standard feminine mule-type slippers with cork heels. As we can see, when she nervously walks towards the front door to open it to Michel, their function is rather to assert her fragility over Nicole's very practical solidity, as exemplified by her slippers. For his part, Michel's footsteps are crisp and hard on the cobbles outside, and upon hearing them Christina's breathing becomes increasingly audible as she panics (later, in the terror sequence, a similar foot tread will trigger her panic once more).

This sequence can be broken down into four temporally uneven parts. The first three parts have a similar distribution of shots (on average, one every 12 seconds or so), but the last part, that of the 'murder' scene, is not only the longest it is also the fastest in terms of editing (on average, one shot every eight seconds).

Diagram 4 – The 'murder' sequence

Part One	Part Two	Part Three	Part Four
Michel enters room gets angry with Christina	Michel tries to reconcile with Christina	Christina spills whisky, Michel gets angry again and then drops off to sleep	Nicole has come in the back way to the bathroom, the two women carry out the drowning Michel
2m40s	1m50s	3m32s	6m25s
13 shots	8 shots	18 shots	50 shots
On average ➤ 1 shot every 12s	➤ 1 shot every 13s	➤ 1 shot every 12s	➤ 1 shot every 8s

Of the four parts, the first is the most complex in terms of camerawork, and it serves to give us a full picture of Nicole's bedroom (see Diagram 5). The camera takes up no fewer than 13 different positions as it shadows Christina and Michel around the room in their very animated quarrel. Although this interior was shot in the studio, the effect is so real because, for a start, the camera takes its various shots from all four walls of the room. Thus, there are three shots from the corridor wall, two from the mantelpiece wall, three from the window wall and five from the double bed/bathroom wall.

Diagram 5 – Nicole's bedroom

	Mantelpiece with lion statue	oval standing-mirror
chest of drawers shepherdess lamp-base		
	round table (with whisky bottle)	
		window
corridor entrance		
		upholstered easy-chair small cupboard with Japanese figurine
		window
	Double-bed with fairly ornate	
Bedside table	foot and headstead Bedside table	bathroom door

The criss-crossing of the camera shots, angled as they are across the room from the various vantage points, reveals how cluttered the space is and picks out details that tell us a bit more about Nicole. The rather pretty porcelain shepherdess lamp-base on the chest of drawers has a cheap and unsuitable lampshade upon it (see the photograph on page 76). The lampshade is all cock-eyed, adding to this sense of neglect or uncaring. Certainly, it is not treated as a piece of feminine adornment within the decor. One assumes that Nicole does not particularly treasure this very feminine object, which in its styling more closely resembles Christina's kind of dress code. The Japanese figurine on the opposite side of the room is also interesting. It is far more clearly visible and shows a woman in a kimono carrying a lantern (could it be a red one?). Undoubtedly, it relates more to Nicole's persona than the shepherdess does! Lying heavily on the mantelpiece is the bronze statue of a reclining lion (supine masculinity one wonders) perched upon some old, lace mantelpiece cover (see photograph on page 77). The clash between masculinity and femininity is virtually unmissable. And when, later, the lion is used (with its great weight) to maintain submerged under water the other embodiment of masculinity (Michel) one senses that all the objects we get to notice have their ironic value. Michel at one point mentions Nicole's great taste, which, understandably, Christina questions, especially when we consider the dark flowered wallpaper and the almost matching upholstered chair. It is not that they are in bad taste per se but they hark back to a much earlier period (the 1910s or early 1920s), showing that the decor has nothing to do with Nicole's taste and far more with her meanness. Nothing has changed in this room, one suspects, since the time when her parents lived there. The only piece of technology she may have introduced is the telephone, even though it is a remarkably old design for the mid-1950s. But what also surprises is that, up until now, we have perceived Nicole as excessively neat and tidy, not given to excess in clothing, accoutrements or adornment. Yet here

View of Nicole's room with shepherdess lamp

she slips into a past where excess is her environment – and she clearly loves it (she says as much several times). The room is nearly bursting at the seams with furniture, and all the furniture is heavy in its materiality, be it wood or fabric. On the one hand, her response consolidates our view of her: as part of the petite bourgeoisie, she would hang onto things. But what is interesting here is that Nicole actually revels in this excess. This suggests that there is more to Nicole than meets the eye. What that is will not be revealed until the end of the film, when we learn that she, like Michel, is driven by greed to kill Christina. We need to recall that this over-stuffed space has all the connotations of decor standing in for repressed desire – something we readily associate with the *mise en scène* in melodrama.[2] In this instance, it refers to Nicole's greed and desire for Michel. So, once again, as with the sunglasses, we have here a clue under our very noses (via the decor) but which we fail to read, this time because so much of the action that is going on in it relates to Christina and Michel's marital conflict and not to Nicole – who is absent for the first three parts of this sequence.

In the first part, Michel comes storming in, shouting at Christina (see photograph on page 78). As he does so he crosses the room, and we catch sight

View of Nicole's room – lion in background

of Christina reacting to his intemperate outburst in the mirror. She jumps with fright and then gestures for him to calm down. During this sequence there are other gestures she uses to express her fear, such as twisting her handkerchief around her fingers in anxiety, or leaning against furniture as if hoping it will hold her up during his onslaught. Interestingly, Vera Clouzot's performance is quite convincing here as she attempts to deal with her menacing husband. But she fails to sustain this moment. Her performance drops off in part two, when her exaggerated response to Michel's dreams of grandeur (raised eyebrows, stark grimaces of disbelief) make her appear awkward and foolish.

The second and third parts of this sequence see-saw between reconciliation and more arguments. They function to intensify the suspense in readiness for murder. There are other layers to what is going on. But it is only with hindsight that we become aware of them and realise that Michel's performance was part of a cat-and-mouse game – where he was the supreme player, pushing and pulling Christina around. From Michel's side there never was any intention of reconciliation. He plays at his game cruelly all the better to batter his wife psychologically – coldly turning a knife in a wound (a form of torture hinted at, as we saw in the previous sequence analysis, by his play

Michel shouts at Christina (pictured in mirror)

with his cigarette holder). As the sequence unfolds, however, we are as unsuspecting of this game as Christina. We are caught up in the suspense of how she will manage to drug Michel, because as far as we and Christina are concerned Michel is doomed. When for a brief moment (in part two) it looks as if Christina is going to waver and be sweet-talked back into a life with her husband, we are again held in suspense; will she spare him? At that moment Michel spots the whisky bottle and demands a glass. Christina does not know, any more than the audience, that Michel is forcing the scheme to murder him forward by asking for this drink. Wanting to believe his promise of a better life and tempted by the idea of a reconciliation, Christina tries to stop him from drinking the spiked whisky. However, she clumsily splashes his suit with the drink and the sweet-talking comes to an abrupt end. For Michel, the slopping of the drink becomes a fortunate accident, because, although he had not foreseen it in his scheming, he can now use it to his advantage. Not only does it help him turn nasty once more, it allows him to be even more convincing in his cruelty; he hits her around the head very hard. Now Christina will feel no compunction in letting him drink himself into oblivion and being drowned in the bath.

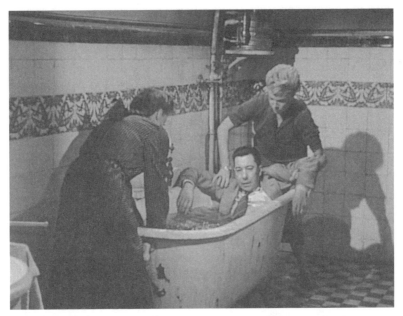

Drowning Michel

Let us now consider the fourth and final part of the sequence. Just as Michel's very noisy performance gave nothing away in the preceding three parts, now Nicole's understated, matter-of-fact, crisp behaviour utterly convinces us that she is seeing this murder through with all the efficiency she can muster. Signoret/Nicole offers a masterful touch when she checks to see if Michel is ready. After lifting his left eyelid she then rubs her finger and thumb together as if they were sullied by what she had just touched. It is only the smallest of gestures (and one which we only get to see because Christina is behind her) but it so cleverly evokes disdain, contempt even, for this man she is about to drown.

From that moment on everything speeds up. The fast-cut feel of this scene is mostly down to the energy Nicole puts into the whole process. Nicole is equally very busy with her own body, adding to this sense of urgency. She rolls up her sleeves, takes off her belt. A lot happens, all dictated by her. She bosses Christina around: 'Burn this,' 'Take his legs,' 'Get the statue' and so on. Christina follows her around more like a shadow than a fully fleshed human being as she gets progressively weaker, and finally she collapses onto the bed. Nicole's energy is matched by her extraordinary strength. Taking the torso end, she literally yanks Michel off the bed. She carries him with ease to the bath, lifts him up and over without much of a struggle, whereas the whole effort of just taking the feet end of the body has nearly killed Christina. Once the body is submerged in the bath, the level of energy does not diminish. Nicole storms back and forth between the two rooms to get the plastic tablecloth, looks over in a reproving way at Christina (who is all but done in), puts the cloth over the bath, crisply slaps down its corners so it looks neat, returns to the bedroom and locks the bathroom door.

Christina's heart condition is not helped by all the physical effort she has had to make in carrying Michel through to the bathroom. But this gets compounded by her taking the leg end, because she is forced to witness Michel's face as he is being drowned. The trauma of this moment is doubled, therefore. And we note the effect on her face as she reacts in horror to Michel's brief but helpless struggle as Nicole pushes him under the water. Her eyes are popping out of her head, and she gasps for air. Meantime, Nicole's face is full of resolve and determination, clearly focused on the job at hand (see photograph on page 79). But Christina can hardly believe what is happening. So, when Nicole asks her to get the bronze statue, she looks bewildered and shakes her head. She simply does not understand the command – she has crossed over into the paralysis of trauma. When she turns and goes to get it she is like an automaton, and behaves similarly when she is instructed to get the tablecloth. Unsurprisingly, she fails to deliver on this last order; there is nothing left, and she just collapses.

During this fourth part there are two cutaways to the tenants upstairs. The first occurs just as Nicole is running the bath and the pipes start to make a terrible din, thus cutting into M. Herboux' enjoyment of his radio quiz show. The second occurs after the murder; all noise has subsided and M. Herboux declares to his long-suffering wife that he will remain awake and seated at his desk until midnight, just in case the two downstairs make any more noise by letting the bathwater out. These diegetic inserts are extremely funny and clash in tone with what has just preceded. This humour cutting into the very dark mood of the moment has a double effect. Because we have knowledge of the murderous activity below, M. Herboux' tantrum at not being able to hear the radio is in some way quite grotesque – 'If only he knew what was going on downstairs,' we mutter to ourselves. And this grotesque moment is capped when M. Herboux ridiculously records the terrible 'crime' of running a bath down into his notebook. Little does he know the real crime. Like his fellow teacher M. Drain before him, he notes but does not understand! His pettiness and petulance at his pleasure being spoilt seem so caricaturally infantile when we consider the seriousness of what is being engineered below. But his reaction also rings so very true, and thus serves to ground events in the real: life does go on 'normally' even while terrible things are happening elsewhere. This cutaway, of course, equally functions to continue the suspense. We would, we believe, rather be downstairs watching what is happening than looking at the antics of this 'silly old fool'. And, just as this insert gives a reality feel in terms of narrative, it also serves to give a sense of real time. Nothing much can happen downstairs while the bath is filling, so this insert fills time (ultimately more interestingly) without drawing attention to the elapse of time itself. Thus, Clouzot has made a clever choice of how to use time and space here that helps add to the feeling of suspense and underlines the utter banality where this crime is concerned.

Finally, this last part, in relation to Nicole, does yield a few clues – which, of course, we overlook, so caught are we in the outward appearance of what is going on (as is M. Herboux). First of all, Nicole comes back too early and begins to draw the bath; the noise awakens and alerts Michel that something is going on. In other words, Nicole almost gives the game away – a carelessness we do not associate with Nicole. In a sense, this is another fortunate accident that Michel turns to his advantage, making his drugging all the more realistic. The idea that Nicole purposefully returns too early, thus making the hoax seem more realistic, does not really work, since Nicole is normally so measured in everything she does. Fortunately, Christina takes control of the situation and reassures Michel that all is well and he should just sleep. However, Nicole's seeming carelessness, had we known how to read it, points, of course, to her confidence in her and Michel's scheme to kill Christina. It shows a lack of subtlety, however, and an eager haste to get on with things. The second clue occurs when Nicole grins at Christina when the latter informs her of the amount of whisky Michel has drunk. We, the audience, are too busy watching her stamp out her cigarette vigorously on the bathroom floor to pay that much attention to her face, so we hear the words more than question the expression on her face – in the context of the apparent narrative, of course she is pleased he has drunk so much because it will make their task easier. However, if we had scrutinised her grin, then we could perhaps have surmised that she is also pleased for him (that he managed to get three

Menacing intruder (shadow in window)

good slugs down before having to endure the next part of their scheme). But the gesture with the cigarette has taken our eye off the ball, so, again, we have missed the clue. Finally, when it is all over, Christina asks Nicole if he might have felt anything. Nicole's response comes rather falteringly, as if she is rather moved by what has happened. Her voice is not strong, nor cold, nor full of confidence but rather hesitant, possibly a little afraid – worried, doubtless, that her lover will have to spend all night in a cold bath.

Terrorising Christina (6m. 40s.)

Part of the secret to the success of terrorising Christina comes down to the ability of the two schemers to use the first-floor space in the school to confuse

Diagram 6 – First floor

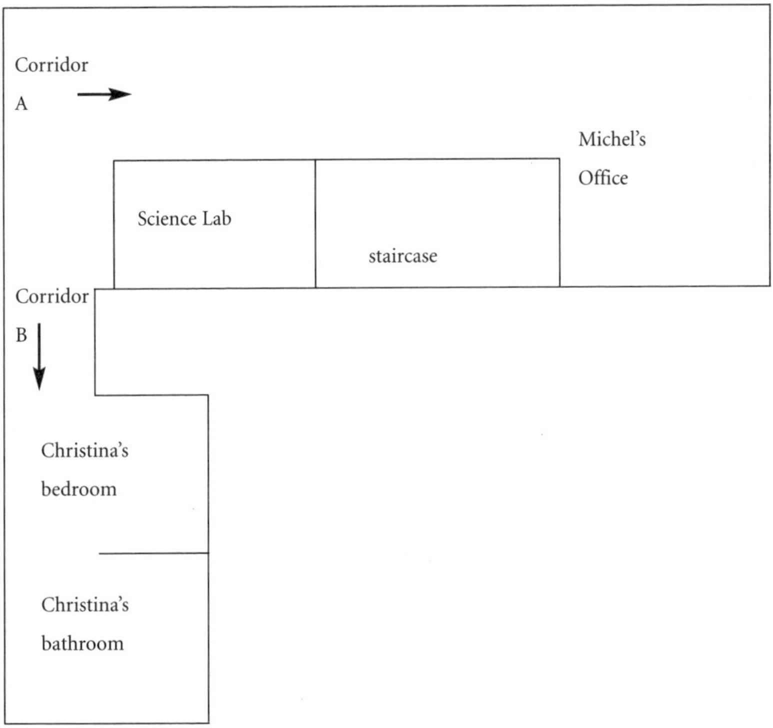

their victim. Diagram 6 will help us understand just how clever they were. First of all, thanks to the editing of the sequence, we get the same impression as Christina that there is only one person moving around the space in a stealthy way (she shouts out: 'Qui est là?/Who's there?' in the singular). Christina sees the shadow of a man in a far window (Michel's office) and she hears his whistling. A bit later, she hears footsteps coming from corridor A, then creaking doors and a clacking typewriter – all of which appear to come from a single source.

Let us now unpick this sequence that leads up to Christina's death and see how the space on the previous page is used. The sequence can be conveniently carved up into four parts, as follows:

Diagram 7

Part One	Part Two	Part Three	Part Four
Christina in her bedroom is awoken by lights going on and off in rooms off corridor A, she sees a shadow in Michel's office	Christina goes down corridor B, she hears footsteps and a door creaking	Christina goes down corridor A, a door creaks, she enters Michel's office, the lights go out, she screams	Christina runs back down corridors A and B to her bedroom, goes to bathroom, discovers Michel in bath, collapses and dies
1m20s	1m20s	2m5s	1m55s
13 shots	11 shots	19 shots	23 shots
On average ➤ 1 shot every 6s	➤ 1 shot every 7s	➤ 1 shot every 7s	➤ 1 shot every 5s

What creates the suspense is not just the sounds – the footsteps, the doors and especially Christina's increasing breathlessness – but the sense, reinforced by the fast editing, that this sinister intruder can appear anywhere. First he appears through a shaft of light downstairs, then we see his gloved hand going up the banister of the staircase (see photographs on page 86). We think it must be Michel (or someone masquerading as him) because of the Prince of Wales suit he is wearing. He then goes all along corridor A, switching lights on and off, ending up in his office (see photograph on page 86). Unbelievably, we hear him whistling. Next he enters into the science lab; we then hear him leaving but are not sure where he has gone. As far as we know, he has somehow got back to the office and has started typing his name incessantly on the typewriter. When Christina enters the office there is no one there, as far as we can determine. It looks as if Michel has disappeared and managed to get down to Christina's bathroom and submerge himself in the water, looking very much like the body she had last seen in the bathroom in Niort.

Only once we get a grip on the topography of this space do we understand how Christina was in fact mesmerised by the sounds (believing what she hears rather than working out the sleights of body). As far as Christina knows, Nicole has left (she has, in fact, just told Fichet that she has gone). So, to her enfeebled mind, the only person who could possibly be generating these various scary noises is either an embodied Michel or his ghost. What really happens is as follows. Once she sees the shadow in Michel's office, Christina decides to investigate. She half runs down corridor B. But just before she gets to the corner of corridors A and B, where the door to the science lab is located (conveniently set within a crenellated recess so that no one can see it from either corridor's direction), Michel enters the lab. Of all ironies, Christina hesitates for a while in front of the lab door (see photograph on page 87). She is facing towards us, her back to the door, clearly unaware of Michel's presence behind the closed door. Her arms are outstretched, holding onto the door jambs; she looks as if she is pinioned there in her terror, martyr-like as if stuck on a cross. She then moves on down corridor A (a fatal mistake!). Meantime, Michel comes out of the lab; Christina hears the door squeak, looks back but does not move. She decides to continue forward, even though the noise was behind her. What appears to tempt her in the forward direction is the shaft of light coming from the slightly ajar door of Michel's office (see photograph page 87). Michel, unbeknown to Christina and, indeed, us, has made off down corridor B towards Christina's bathroom. What has also muddled Christina's perceptions is the sound of the typewriter, which now begins to clack away fast and hard. We, like Christina,

Menacing Intruder (shadow)

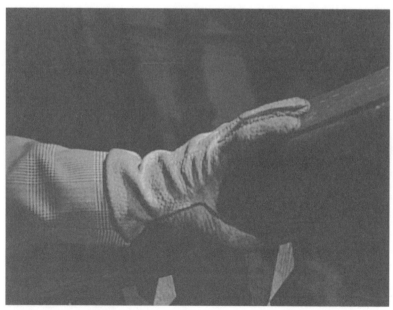

Menacing intruder (gloved hand)

Terrorised Christina in front of lab door

Christina approaches Michel's office

Christina in terror

Menacing intruder (shadow of hand)

The monstrous Michel rises from the dead

Christina is finally dead

are seduced into thinking it is Michel – even though the logic of movement in time and space tells us it cannot be. So, when Christina advances to the door and it gradually opens, throwing more and more light onto her, small wonder her face is frozen in terror and her eyes are tightly shut, because she is almost convinced that Michel or his dead ghost will pounce on her (see photograph on page 88). We too believe that he is still there, since we see the shadow of a hand moving across to the light switch (see photograph on page 88). But, when the light snaps off and Christina screams in terror and runs back to her own quarters, there clearly is not time enough for Michel to get to the bathroom before her. The reason we believe that it is all Michel's doing comes back to Clouzot's skilful play with space in the opening sequence, where, as already mentioned, space seems confined and quickly traversed. Our perceptions are as erroneous as Christina's. In fact, the person doing the business in Michel's office is, of course, Nicole. She it is who types so crisply and with such speed – without a single error, it has to be said! It is she who cynically sets the scene with Michel's gloves and fedora hat around the typewriter – almost like the cover of a crime novel! It is she who slowly opens the door to let the shaft of light fall on Christina. Finally, it is she whose hand we see in the shadow and which switches off the light. Thus, we have been duped. All the time we had believed with Christina that either there was no one in the room or that it had to be Michel or his ghost – whereas, in fact, it was Nicole, unseen, hiding behind the door. An astute game of terror, all of which depended on timing and the assumption that Christina was by now so traumatised that she would not be able to think rationally.

All that is needed now is the icing on the cake of this horrible and diabolical plot. And this comes in the form of Michel's emergence from the bath (see photograph on page 89). The past is re-enacted, but in reverse: this time Michel rises from the dead. His eyes appear to have rolled back, showing only the whites and making him appear spectral, monstrous to Christina, who crumples helplessly in a heap on the floor (see photograph on page 89).[3]

In Chapter 3, I discussed briefly Christina's desperate urge to investigate the shadow and the sounds to which she has borne witness. I suggested that her response was typical of a person who is caught in trauma. In this last part of the film, she is awoken from her dreams twice – once by Fichet lighting his cigarette from a candle, the second time by the lights being switched on and off in the rooms along corridor A. In both instances the source of her awakening is light. Arguably, dreams reflect the desire of the consciousness not to wake up. Indeed, Sigmund Freud states that 'the dream is the guardian of sleep not its disturber'.[4] But what happens if those dreams are clearly nightmares – as is the case for Christina? Freud, in his discussion of the father who desperately wants to hold onto sleep while his dead child keeps trying to awaken him, argues that dreams also function as the ethical imperative to be awake – to witness the fact of death. So the light, in Christina's case, causes an awakening, albeit against the very wishes of the consciousness, forcing a confrontation with a reality she cannot escape. She has to be enlightened. The awakening itself becomes the site of trauma, forcing her into what Jacques Lacan calls the trauma of the necessity and impossibility of responding to another's death.[5] In Christina's case we can see how she struggles with this awakening, because on the two occasions that it occurs she is forced to confront her own implication in that death (i.e. Michel's). She tells Fichet the truth ('I killed him') and she persists in trying to find the source of the noises ('Who's there?'). No one will believe her – Fichet dismisses her confession and the shadow continually eludes her – so she must find the corpse, to confirm her guilt and pass the knowledge onto others. Only through the body can she awaken others to the truth. The terrible pathos of this gesture is that she will be believed, and her knowledge will be passed on, *only* when she is dead. However, this knowledge is not of Michel's murder, but of her own death – only through her own corporeal ending is the truth finally out. Too late for her, Fichet steps in on Nicole and Michel celebrating the success of their scheme to kill Christina and he exposes their heinous crime. As if to stress even further how horrible the scheming duo were, Christina's own physical fragility is quite rawly underlined by the fact that, when she runs down the corridors, we can clearly see her bodily form through the transparent fabric of her nightie. We can see her breasts and nipples, see the curve of her hips and the shapeliness of her legs through the lightweight cotton. Her body is as fragile and as translucent as the fabric that covers it, almost as if only once we see through her body can we understand the enigma of this devilish plot – 'in corpora veritas' as M. Drain might have said!

Notes

1   The headline of the article Nicole is reading is probably not innocent – 'Le long du rideau de fer les paysans ne fauchent plus l'herbe/behind the Iron Curtain the peasants no longer scythe their grass' – and there is a photograph of what looks like a combine harvester. We learn later that Nicole gets her own papers delivered; clearly, she likes to be abreast of the news. Petite bourgeoise she might be but not so provincial as not to want to be informed about what is going on behind the Iron Curtain. And, mindful of the mood of censorship during this period of the 1950s and Clouzot's own comments about it, we have to conjecture that either Clouzot or Signoret wanted at least to have the pleasure of knowing that the fleeting headline was in the film – pointing to the fact that Communist countries were modernising their agriculture (even more rapidly than the French).

2   See Geoffrey Nowell-Smith's comments on the function of decor; Nowell-Smith, Geoffrey (1987), pp. 73–74.

3   Bocquet (1993), p. 91 cites Meurisse's anecdote about the rolled eyes. Apparently, Meurisse was incapable of rolling his eyes back so all one could see were the whites of his eyes. When Clouzot tartly remarked that Cécile Aubry could, Meurisse came back, with: 'Perhaps it is better to have talent than to know how to roll one's eyes!' as a retort. Determined to have the last word, Clouzot announced that he would have to wear white contact lenses. Meurisse uses these props to good effect in the scene, since it is quite horrible to watch him in close-up as he slowly slips them out of his eyes!

4   Freud, Sigmund (1953), p. 267. For a very useful study of dreams and trauma, see Caruth, Cathy (1995), pp. 89–108. I am indebted to her analysis of Freud's account of a father who has lost his child and Lacan's subsequent reinterpretation of this dream.

5   See Caruth (1995), p. 96.

5   Not even reinventing the wheel: the 1996 remake – *Diabolique*

There have been several remakes of *Les Diaboliques*, but arguably the most notorious one is Jeremiah Chechik's 1996 *Diabolique,* starring Sharon Stone as Nicole and Isabelle Adjani as Mia (a renamed Christina). Chazz Paliminteri plays Guy Baran, the vicious husband. I say 'notorious' because of the controversy surrounding its excessive borrowing from the Clouzot original and because of its claim to have remained 'emotionally truer to the book' by reinserting the supposedly missing lesbian text.[1]

The title should be the first alarm bell. If this film does not refer to Clouzot's, why use the same US release title of 1955? The duplication of the title makes one immediately suspicious as to its referent, especially since it was only the alternative title to the one that was more commonly used, *The Diabolical Ones*. Why select the more obscure title? Why drop the definite article and the plural of the original (*Les Diaboliques*)? The question becomes 'what does Chechik's title refer to?', not to whom, since the term is here an adjective, not a noun. So, is the situation diabolical? The plot? One of the characters, through his/her behaviour? If the female focus is an essential ingredient of this film then why not use the plural? Titles get recycled all the time in the film industry. The title, then, seems to lead nowhere. A second alarm bell rings. Since earlier remakes had at least had the temerity to offer new titles (the TV film *Reflections of Murder*, 1974, and *House of Secrets*, 1993), why actually draw attention to oneself by using such a derivative title? Henri-Georges Clouzot's widow Inès Clouzot was, quite rightly, alerted to the possible copycat nature of Chechik's film once she heard of its title, and could hardly be blamed for taking legal action to ban the film worldwide. She did, after all, own the rights to the original film. Why then did Morgan Creek (the production company) claim that the film was based on Boileau and Narcejac's novel (which anyone can see is patently not true!) and later revise their story, insisting that they had bought the rights to both the novel and the film? By this stage even Sharon Stone was becoming embarrassed,[2] and the story as smelly as the fish that Michel tried to force down his wife's throat!

In fact, the remake does borrow very heavily from Clouzot's adaptation, and there is even less of the original novel in Chechik's version than the 1955 one. What had happened in terms of authors' rights was that Morgan Creek had bought them from Warner Bros, who had themselves obtained the rights from the American TV station ABC (it was they who had made the 1974 TV film). The problem, in terms of clarity of ownership, comes down to this signing to ABC, which took place in 1972. Somehow, when the rights to the novel were sold, an intermediary on the chain of agents managed to slip in a clause lifting the ban on a remake of Clouzot's film. However, he never held the legal right to do this. So, when Morgan Creek claimed that Clouzot had sold the rights clandestinely, they were quite wrong. His widow's retort came quick and fast. She accused them of being misinformed and of preferring to plunder her husband's film because it was better than the novel. In the end the furore over the release was resolved. Inès Clouzot received financial compensation (to the tune of £75,000) and the right to exhibit the original film freely four months after the release of the American remake.[3]

Briefly, to make the point of how lacking in originality Chechik's remake is, we can note that the film is set in a private boys' boarding school, the two women drive to Philadelphia to Nicole's house to carry out the murder (drowning in the bath), Nicole has snoopy neighbours (living below, this time), Nicole and Mia return to the school and throw Guy's body into the swimming pool, the body disappears, ghostly events occur that terrorise Mia (much the same as in Clouzot's film, with a little updating of the technology), Guy's body reappears in the bath and he almost succeeds in killing Mia (through a heart attack). The only difference (and it is drastic) is the dénouement: Mia and Nicole manage finally to drown Guy in the swimming pool after a terrible fight.

While it is quite easy to discredit Chechik's remake as a very poor imitation of the Clouzot film, *Diabolique* did not sink without a trace. In its first weekend release in the United States it made $5.7 million, so clearly American audiences were drawn to something: most likely the image of Sharon Stone, who had had a blistering hit with *Basic Instinct* (1992). Maybe the promise of a lesbian subplot in *Diabolique* created an anticipation of more sexual erotics from this woman, who had so controversially played a bisexual in the earlier film. Seeing her at play with Isabelle Adjani (another interesting erotic body and one readily associated with sexual hysteria) probably made the prospect even more appetising.

There are, however, three basic flaws with the remake. First, there are too many twists in the plot, so the narrative thread gets very thin and difficult to follow. Second, the two main female characters lack substance and therefore bring very little credibility to their roles. Finally, the lesbian plot is as unconvincing in its presence as is the claim by Morgan Creek and Chechik that they were putting back into the film what Clouzot had taken out in terms of the relationship between the two women.[4]

Chechik's film is a queer hybrid between Clouzot's film and Boileau and Narcejac's novel. For the most part it stays very close to the former, but on three occasions it veers off the Clouzot trail and heads towards the latter text in its suggestion of lesbian moments – even though these are moments that do not, incidentally, have any direct referent within the original Boileau and Narcejac narrative. The first disassociation, interestingly, reveals the basic problem with the film, namely that there are too many loose threads. When Guy's suit and a roll of film turn up containing photographs of the two women with the wicker trunk, Nicole reckons a blackmailer is at work. She then reveals to Mia that her reason for killing Guy was to get her hands on the money he had embezzled from his wife. It is good that we know this, since nothing prior to this moment in Nicole's behaviour with Guy would lead us to any other conclusion than that she is having a very sexy affair with him. Mia is outraged to find out she has been the victim of fraud. Nicole doubles the dose and confesses that the original plot was to get rid of her; but she insists that because Guy double-crossed her she wants to side with Mia. By now things have escalated into an argument; the two women fight over who killed Guy. Mia declares she will tell the police that she and Nicole were lovers and that Nicole killed Guy out of jealousy. 'Wow!' says Nicole. 'You *can* take the girl out of the convent!' Whatever can have occurred before in that relationship to provoke Mia into making such a declaration (that they were lovers)? Furthermore, what do we make of the fact that we are told in this sequence that the reason Guy had decided to act alone was because he thought Nicole and Mia were lovers? Where did that come from? Something in the behaviour between the two women must have suggested that they were possibly an item. There are two hints. At one point Nicole caresses Mia and asks her if Guy does this sort of thing to her when they make love. However, while it is an erotically charged moment, Nicole is actually using it to diminish Mia as a sexual partner to Guy (indeed, later she says, cattily, 'I'm not surprised he comes to me after you'). The other hint occurs just after the murder; the two women are in bed and the sleeping Mia rests her arm over the awake Nicole. These moments, then, are tossed into the narrative to point to the original lesbian narrative. But neither really works, the first because it is used in spite, the second because it has no narrative justification for being there. Furthermore, the fact remains that Guy is never privy to these moments, so how could he imagine that they are lovers? Thus, these suggestive hints are only there for us the audience. While they might be there to titillate, all they do in fact is serve to confuse. Up until now we have seen both women having consensual sex with Guy, seemingly actively craving it. So what are we to make of these lesbian moments? Will the film now develop the lesbian plot? No such thing. The narrative returns to the Clouzot masterprint. Mia goes to the police hoping to identify her husband, and she gets stuck with a retired police inspector Shirley Vogel (Kathy Bates) who will not take no for an answer.

But then a new development occurs when a pregnant mistress turns up at the school and demands money for an abortion. The plot twists again – a second disassociation that sends it back to the lesbian text. Nicole knew nothing of this affair, but Mia did, although she said nothing to Nicole because she did not want her to be hurt! Within a matter of minutes, however, Mia tells Nicole she has to go because 'I am sick of you'. Nicole leaves, visibly distressed as she drives off in the rain. When fumbling in her handbag for a cigarette she comes across a wad of money that Mia has obviously put there. She had intended to leave Mia to her fate (the bathroom scene where Guy returns and, like Lazarus, raises himself from the bath). But now she decides to return and rescue Mia. This is the third return to the lesbian text. Eventually she manages to save Mia (after some fairly horrific fighting, in which Mia also rescues her). The film ends with Nicole and Mia saying goodbye to each other.

In other words, whereas in Clouzot's film the dynamic between the two women is the core that gives some sense of depth to the film, in Chechik's version any suggestion that there might be a lesbian link between the two women is so artificially contrived, so heavily flagged up (even to the point of the two men who are making a promotion video for the school declaring that they must be dykes), that it gets in the way of the plot development. Furthermore, it bears no relevance to the original novel.

Casting and characterisation are also problematic in Chechik's film. While Stone carries her role well enough as the updated Nicole and undoubtedly is paying homage to her earlier embodiment through Simone Signoret, there are qualitative differences of note. The most evident one is the dress code. Whereas Signoret's Nicole had been understated, Stone's draws attention to itself throughout the first two-thirds of the film (until Mia goes to the police) with her brightly coloured retro 1950s costumes (designed by L'wren Scott). To Signoret's black, grey and drab (to say nothing of the carpet slippers) we have Stone's lime green and red. Each time Stone enters the frame she is in a different outfit (more a fashion plate than a scheming murderer), so there is an aura of excess, which is visually represented in relation to her character (as opposed to the more psychological depths of excess associated with Signoret's Nicole). We also have the red gash of lipstick and the hard red nails. Signoret's Nicole wears neither lipstick nor nail polish – another instance of her not drawing attention to herself as a femme fatale. Bizarrely, once Shirley Vogel turns up – who, in her attire, would make drab look chic – Stone begins to wear brown tailored suits and black dresses. She also seems to have forgone the sunglasses, for the most part, in favour of a pair of reading glasses (to assert her role as a teacher, doubtless), which now adorn her nose or her chest (since they are on a chain). We begin to see her in the classroom. In other words, she has neutered her role as the visible femme fatale by taming down the colour of her dress code and swapping her glasses. But why? There is no law of the father coming in, in the form of the ex-police inspector, to restore order and contain the femme fatale, since Vogel is a woman. Has Nicole decided that by becoming neutral she can hedge her bets better? Deny her earlier masquerade as the femme fatale? She does, after all, have several changes of heart. Or has she shifted over into the dark colour camp, which more readily identifies her with Mia, who – for the most part – is dressed in grungy browns? In other words, by masquerading in the opposite direction (becoming Mia-like, neutering her femme fatale status) – a double masquerade indeed – has she 'gone over'? By queering her look, is she trying to hide away in the female land of drabness? Whatever the case, the shift is so radical that it represents yet another element that draws attention to itself, like the dotting of the plot with lesbian moments, again pointing to the struggle of this film to secure what it is trying to be.

As for Adjani, one can only feel tremendous sympathy for both the miscasting of her in this role and the cruel attempts to deny her any sense of style! As Geoff Andrew puts it, there is little scope for her 'to deliver the raw emotion she is so good at'.[5] Typically, an Adjani performance is on the very edge of hysteria, and yet here she is expected to be repressed, contained, fearful and terrorised – the very opposite of her performative self. She wears terrible clothes; dresses that, for the most part, look like schoolgirl tunics (and as if made from felt cloth – perhaps the closest she could get to a hair shirt, one suspects!). Only once does she get to wear virginal white, and that is the moment when the two guys making the video accuse her and Nicole of being dykes – so that worked well as asserting heterosexual femininity! This was also one of the rare moments when she sported sunglasses, matching her up to Nicole. Her hair is a disgrace, like a waist-length curtain, behind which she hides. There is something of the durgeful Gothic about her. It is very clear that she is acting as a foil for Stone's more energetic and glamour-filled performance. She is droopy, weak, childish, given to running to the confessional. This is why the closing sequence has such tremendous shock value – and is ultimately pretty unbelievable. Wherever did she get the strength to throw herself into the swimming pool and help rescue Nicole by drowning Guy? We are amazed. What happened to her weak heart? Here, at last, is the old Adjani we know, the Reine Margot who is an assertive, highly sexualised woman and equally unafraid of the many threats to her safety. But that Adjani is not allowed to expose herself for long. Pretty quickly she is feeling terrible about what has happened and bids adieu to Nicole as she (probably) makes her way to the confessional, despite Shirley Vogel announcing that Guy's death by drowning was self-defence.

In the end, Chechik's film achieves the every opposite of what it purported to do. And, as such, it deserves to be seen as an anti-feminist, backlash film. In no way does it serve the original lesbian text, nor does it assert a place for the relationship between the two women. Even the weak attempt at female solidarity, via the Kathy Bates character of the female detective (who makes it clear she is going to turn a blind eye to the truth of the murder), fails to convince us that we are watching anything other than a chauvinistic film. Kim Newman in his review sums it up well when he says that Chechik's film

> seems to go out of its way to show them in a [literal] bad light. The lesbian undertones of the original [Clouzot film] are almost overtones here, as the murderesses exchange cuddles in extremis. Adding to the feminist duo but also extending the film's woman-hating is Kathy Bates' Columboesque PI, who tosses off jaw-droppingly atrocious jokes about her character's mastectomy and someone else's Aids. [6]

In short, where Chechik's film is concerned, Mme Clouzot need not have troubled herself; it is not even a shadow of the earlier film, just diabolically bad.

Notes

1   Chechik, Jeremiah, quoted in Mayne (2000), p. 61.
2   See *Première* 4 (4), 1996, p. 4.
3   All the details of this sorry affair can be found in the following publications: *Le Film français*, 1 March 1996, p. 9; *Le Film Français*, 29 March 1996, p. 4; and *Première* 4 (4), 1996, p. 4.
4   Chechik, quoted in Mayne (2000), p. 61.
5   Andrew, Geoff (2001), p. 276.
6   Newman, Kim, Review of *Diabolique*, *Sight and Sound* 6 (9), 1996, p. 39.

6 Critical reception of *Les Diaboliques*

Les Diaboliques was a great hit. It was premiered on 29 January 1955 at the Gaumont-Palace Berlitz (the biggest cinema theatre in Europe at that time, with 4,670 seats), where it had an exclusive run for 17 weeks. In terms of the final audience figures for 1955, it came seventh. The top-grossing film of the year was *Le Comte de Monte Cristo* (7.7 million spectators). During *Les Diaboliques'* actual run, however, it came second to Sacha Guitry's extremely expensive colour extravaganza *Napoléon* (which ran 23 weeks in exclusivity and came second overall with 5.4 million). Other statistics provide some interesting information.[1] In terms of audience preferences, *Les Diaboliques* was the front runner in Paris, but elsewhere, in the provinces, it came second or fourth to *Napoléon*.[2] Traditionally it is the case that thrillers do better in Paris than in the provinces, so in some respects these rankings are quite strong. Clouzot's film did least well in the southern provincial towns of Marseilles and Toulouse (where it came sixth and seventh respectively). *Napoléon*'s trajectory was the reverse, in that it came top and doubled its Paris figures in the provinces.[3] Given Clouzot's reputation for his hatred of small-town provincial mentalities (first gained with *Le Corbeau*) it could be said he was fortunate not to reap what he sowed in terms of audience disaffection (with the exception of Marseilles and Toulouse). But, clearly, these audiences wanted to be elevated both by the grandiose image of one of France's national heroes, Napoleon, and his embodiment by another 'great man' (Sacha Guitry himself), and to be almost frightened to death by Clouzot's diabolical fiends.

The scope of this chapter's overview takes on board contemporary reviews of Clouzot's film *Les Diaboliques* in the critical and trade presses of France, the United Kingdom and the United States. Reception immediately after the film's release was mixed. In France, in the critical journals *Cahiers du cinéma* and *Positif*, opinion was divided. In the daily press, the communist newspaper *L'Humanité* condemned the film, but the centre-left *Le Monde* praised it. The French trade papers (*Le Cinéma français, La Cinématographie française* and *Le Film français*) unanimously sang its praises. In the United Kingdom, both *Sight and Sound* and *The Monthly Film Bulletin* remained unimpressed, as did the daily press. The UK trade press, however, universally acclaimed the film, as indeed did most of the American trade papers, with the exception of *Variety*.

Cahiers du cinéma and questions of genre

Intriguingly, there were three separate, consecutive reviews of *Les Diaboliques* in *Cahiers du cinéma*. The first, by André Bazin, appeared in the January 1955 issue, the second, by Jacques Audiberti, in February and the last, by Jean-Louis Tallenay, in March. Given that Clouzot was not in the *Cahiers'* hall of auteurs it is interesting that so much space should have been devoted to his film. The three articles are interlinked; whether this was intentional or not is unclear, since they do not make reference to each other. All three take on board the question of genre – more specifically, the noir thriller/polar genre. Interestingly, in terms of critical film theory during that period, it was Bazin who felt that genre should be as much a part of the film debates as auteurism. He did not particularly like the single focus on the auteur. So, in this context, these three articles make for an extraordinary conjunction, a moment of genre theory in the wilderness of auteur theory. And that in itself makes *Les Diaboliques* remarkable: the film of an interloper (a representative of Truffaut's hated *cinéma de papa*) advancing genre theory; how could that be? Bazin's article, 'Le style c'est le genre/Style is genre', essentially makes the point that Clouzot's film is a perfect exercise in style and, as such, runs true to the film genre. In this regard, Bazin declares, it is his most perfect film. However, he also judges it to be a minor film, and for the following reasons. Because it runs so true to type, the characters themselves also run to type and lack psychological depth. And, because it runs to type, the film is only pure style. Thus, in Bazin's view, when the film comes to its end (with Moinet declaring he has seen Christina) a new film could very easily be born out of this revelation – after all, when Moinet said that Michel was still alive, it turned out to be true, so why not the same for Christina? In its ending, the film reveals its true weakness. There is no substance; another film could replace it.[4]

The third review, by Tallenay, seems to pick up on this idea. His entire review is based on an absurdist approach whereby he proposes to critique the film by reconstructing an imaginary one. In this way he will demonstrate how the sparkling style hides the inevitable emptiness of the film. Thus, Tallenay suggests (in his new scenario) that, when Christina dies, we are only halfway through the film. Thereafter it transpires that she has colluded with the inspector to pretend to die so as to expose Nicole and Michel's dastardly scheme to kill her. The inspector has managed to substitute Christina's supposed corpse for another at the morgue. However, Christina deliberately fails to turn up at the trial and Nicole is sentenced to death. The detective is forced to denounce Christina. Nicole and Michel are set free. But the trio are now wanted for all kinds of breaches of the law and make their escape on a liner to Latin America. And so on ad infinitum.[5] The irony should not be lost here that, in his remake, Chichek attempted – albeit in a different way – to change the ending and let Christina live, but that he singularly failed to make it convincing (see previous chapter).

Both Bazin and Tallenay, while readily conceding that they like Clouzot's film, nonetheless appear to reproach Clouzot for following the codes and conventions of the thriller genre too closely. Bazin also goes on to accuse Clouzot of playing a cat-and-mouse game with his audience (something that, arguably, Hitchcock does as part of his humour). With all the twists and turns in the plot Clouzot 'is intentionally playing with our nerves,' declares Bazin.[6] We fall into the trap of believing what we hear and see. We are so worn out, says Bazin, small wonder we are hugely relieved when at the end all is unveiled for us – no matter how realistic it is. In all of this, Bazin concedes, Clouzot has played the genre's specificities to perfection. However, he seems to imply that Clouzot adds nothing to the genre. Even the introduction of the inspector adds nothing, as he remains surplus to requirement[7] – a view shared, incidentally, by the second film critic, Audiberti.[8]

It is this idea of emptiness that intrigues me, because I believe the critics have a point but that they are pointing in the wrong direction. All the images in Clouzot's film are insecure, capable of lying. Equally, the characters, as bearers of masks, are unreadable. We know only that Michel is a tyrannical bully, certainly not that he is a killer. As for Nicole, she too bears her mask well. It is our inability (or laziness) to measure and investigate her that leads us astray. With all the play with masks and mirrors we lose our way, end up probing the wrong things, situations or people. And wherever we do probe we come out empty-handed. How difficult it is to make things stick, especially if we cannot, or choose not to, penetrate beyond the surface. Do we wish to know about the sordid perversions of others? In witnessing them, do we not wish to be spared looking into the mirror that could so easily reflect us? So, this emptiness is not so much the 'Clouzot effect' as it is the *affect* of his films, in this instance *Les Diaboliques*. He loves to show us that which is not, to conceal that which is. So here, in this context, it is a murder 'which is not' and yet which will cause a death. In this emptiness, which is, of course, so full (everything is there if only we could see it, as we saw in our sequence analyses), in this emptiness, which is an emptying out, we are looking at the degree zero of the noir thriller; indeed, even its death as we know it. So Clouzot is actually doing something new with this genre after all.

Let us look further. Whereas in film noir the central protagonist is a flawed character, Clouzot makes no excuses for his. His characters are driven, which is why, in his films, action (namely the body) counts more than motive (the mind). Similarly, love is a driving force rather than an emotion in his narratives. In Clouzot's films the line between good and evil, black and white, truth and falsehood, is indecipherable. In life, human hypocrisy tries to hide this ambiguity, to suppress its reality. There is no line, according to Clouzot; we are that ambiguity embodied.[9] All actions are double-edged, as *Les Diaboliques* makes so clear. So, if we, the audience, become anxious in watching this film, if we feel we have been duped, this is not – strictly speaking – because Clouzot has tricked us (since he has given us the information), but because we have failed to read the signs. And this is what makes his contribution to the genre so interesting. Clouzot suggests always that there is off-screen space, but we seem to forget about it. If we had only thought a bit more laterally (rather than literally) we could have worked out, for example, that in the final sequence Nicole probably has not left the school (we only have Christina's word for it, and she is in bed so can hardly have verified it for herself). We accept the word before the action, and because of that we end up identifying with Christina. If we had been sharper-witted we might have seen the ambiguity of things more clearly. What I am proposing here is a second complementary aspect of Clouzot's contribution to the film noir genre, namely audience participation. His work suggests that we need to work. If we remain passive recipients then we will live the drama at one level, the one of misrecognition and error. If, however, we drop our own masks, willingly engage with the mirrors, think laterally, then we will be more actively engaged in the narrative, be part of the levels of meaning production. This seems quite radical as filmmaking practice, surely making Clouzot worthy of the label of 'auteur'. Finally, on this idea of tricking the audience, Clouzot, arguably, was the first to do so in the noir thriller. As such, he becomes the inventor of the psychological twist that renders the text and narrative unstable – a practice that was deeply influential on Hitchcock (*Vertigo*) and later films, such as the Japrisot adaptations (*The Usual Suspects*, Bryan Singer, 1995, and *Nine Queens*, Fabian Bielinsky, 2002).[10]

International reviews

The British trade review *Kinematograph Weekly* raises an interesting issue, which several papers run with and which points to the way in which a film changes in nature once it is exported – especially if it is a foreign-language film. Apparently, the British Board of Censors issued *Les Diaboliques/The Fiends* with an 'X' certificate because of the drowning scene.[11] The scene was shot in full camera view, so, clearly, the film could not constitute family viewing. *The Daily Mirror*, rather unfairly, uses this particular film to excoriate the plethora of 'foreign' 'X'-rated films that were preventing nice family outings to the cinema. The editor of this article goes on to suggest that this film offers a 'suspenseful but sordid slice of French life'.[12] It is almost as if the fact of having an 'X' certificate means that this film must be undesirable because implicitly it can be associated with other films of its 'X' ilk, where 'brutality becomes more blatant, sex more stark, and the horrors more gruesome'.[13] Yet there is very little physical brutality in this film, no sex, and the horrors are more in the mind than elsewhere. The editor of another

British newspaper, *Tribune*, goes further, and having fumed against 'foreign' films for their salaciousness he goes on to state that 'the calculated vileness of *The Fiends* is a whore of a different colour. A sadistic schoolmaster, his rich ailing wife, and her Lesbian friend, who is also the schoolmaster's mistress, continue their *ménage-à-trois* from bickering and bullying, to drugging and drowning.'[14] Curiously, in invoking the 'Lesbian friend', the editor manages to alight on something that Clouzot had spent considerable energy trying to remove from his film. It is as if, for this newspaper at least, the 'X' sign means there has to be some 'filth' somewhere, if not in sex per se then in its queerness ('a whore of a different colour'). Thus, we can see how, despite the fact that the text remains the same (i.e., it has not changed since it left the shores of France), the censorship sign can serve to bring about a different reading of the filmic text, even to the point of seeing things that are not actually present. An odd effect of film exporting (and British puritanism) if ever there was one.

Nor was the popular press alone in rejecting this film for its supposed sordidness (meant here in a sexual and moral sense). *Sight and Sound* and *The Monthly Film Bulletin*, both of which are far from prudish, experienced Clouzot's film, respectively, as a passionless drama that was nonetheless 'soggy with sexual perversion'[15] and a film with an 'implausible trick ending' coupled with an 'equivocal relationship between the two women'.[16] These two reviews seem to be attacking the film not just for its lack of verisimilitude, although that is part of it, but for its merciless view of marriage, which, according to *Sight and Sound,* would be more appropriate in a melodrama set in the 19th century – a point, incidentally, with which the American trade journal *Variety* concurs.[17]

The British trade papers seem alone in having managed to get behind the morality smokescreen outlined above and come at Clouzot's film with a degree of freshness and appreciation for his craft. Thus, *To-day's Cinema* and *The Daily Film Renter* speak of the effective way in which Clouzot uses contrast to create a realism effect. *To-day's Cinema* comments on 'the great director's talents' and how he 'gets his effects by the constant contrast of horror and seedy normality'.[18] *The Daily Film Renter*, for its part, refers to the contrast between the actual narrative and the 'effective use of a technique as seemingly realistic as if the film were a straight documentary', an effect that is enhanced by 'the natural sound effects' and a lack of background music.[19]

The American *The Film Daily* also recognises Clouzot as 'a master of movie technique', so that, for this trade paper too, the 'overall effect is gripping'.[20] Essentially, the English-speaking trade papers were taken with the realism of the film – almost, it has to be said, to the same degree that the critical journals were not. In some ways this is fortunate, since trade papers influence distribution and exhibition. But the gap is of interest and merits a brief comment. For *The Monthly Film Bulletin* everything is wrong with the film, starting with the pacing. The film is too long, too slow, the tricks of suspense get in the way of psychological development. The central section (where, as we saw, in Chapter 2, the two women appear to be in control), which builds up 'the equivocal relationship between the two women', is too lumbering and 'over-weights the situation without materially advancing it'.[21] One wonders finally if it is not the 'equivocal nature of the relationship between the two women' that is the overriding problem here, for the criticism of slow pacing does not really hold. We have already noted that Clouzot's film is fast-paced (especially for a French film). It is also the case that thrillers rarely develop the psychological aspect of their characters – a lack that paradoxically, gives pace to the genre. However, Clouzot's film was labelled a 'psychological thriller' and considerable depth is given to both Nicole and Michel's characterisations, as we have suggested in previous chapters. So, there is psychological development, despite *The Monthly Film Bulletin*'s criticism – a feature that could have led to the film appearing to be slow (even though, technically speaking, it is not). As a final retort to *The Monthly Film Bulletin*'s dislike of the film, we have seen how the suspense is tight and claustrophobic and how, according to trade journal *The Film Daily*, these moments are subtly dotted along the narrative rather than self-reflexively drawing attention to themselves. The perceived gap between craft and content that some reviewers have commented upon so unfavourably could, then, have something to do with a clash in their minds between representation and characterisation. In their view, there is, apparently, a lack of propriety in two women getting close, plotting and carrying out a murder and then trying to keep their crime concealed at the same time as they endeavour to unearth the missing corpse. It unbalances the narrative line, according to these critics. Necrophilia, to say nothing of equivocal (queer) relationships, is, doubtless, an unseemly domain for women.

Accentuating the positive: performances to die for

If we leave aside the daily paper *L'Humanité*, which was so disparaging about the film, calling it retrograde and formulaic and its characters unbelievable,[22] where there is consensus among our critics is in the realm of performance. Signoret and Meurisse are singled out for their tremendously powerful renditions of the mendacious schemers. Charles Vanel's cameo is remarked upon, and even Vera Clouzot gets some flattering comments. *L'Humanité Dimanche* was in kinder mood than her sister daily, finding the performances excellent despite the film being only a brilliant 'exercise de style'.[23] *Tribune* (which will be remembered for its loathing of the film) comments upon the 'remarkable acting of the three principals'.[24] *The Monthly Film Bulletin*, also no fan of the film, grudgingly concedes that Clouzot is 'competently served by his players'.[25] It is, of course, possible to appreciate the acting and not like the film. But, since the film has been criticised, by a number of the critics we have discussed, both for its style and content – either for having too much style and no content or for the content being perverse – and yet still appreciated for the acting, we have to assume that the film remains something of a paradox for them. Quite possibly it is the characters' inability to elicit any sympathy among these critics, a point made by Penelope Houston in her review,[26] that alienates them from the film text. After all, stars reach us through their bodies, are the vehicles for genre as much as the genre is their vehicle. The suggestion is, then, that the stars' performance kept these critics at a distance, making the viewing temperature rather cold, thus allowing them to perceive the contrivances and 'perversions' of the film's plot as just that.

While the tension Clouzot sought to achieve did not happen for them, on the contrary, *The Daily Film Renter* felt it was all there and, indeed, 'increased by the first rate acting of the stars'.[27] Moreover, other critics were far from being unaffected by the performances.[28] Both *The Film Daily* and *La Cinématographie française* were deeply moved by Vera Clouzot's performance. Meurisse's ability to suggest rather than show violence is commented upon by *Kinematograph Weekly* as a powerful aspect of his performance strategy, and the critic mentions by way of example the scene in which Michel forces his wife to eat the rotten fish.[29] Indeed, we can almost feel the slime of the fish in our own mouths as Christina cringingly submits to his despicable behaviour. There is a chilling ferocity that emanates from his body and his speech. His voice is authoritarian, hard, heavily dosed with cynicism; he exudes refined violence.

However, *the* star persona who gets the greatest coverage, by far, is Signoret – unsurprisingly, in a way, since she is the linchpin to the whole drama. The other reason, of course, is that her performance has enormous depth. She seems to come from somewhere; she is not a mere cipher for the current thriller. She has a past. Above all, she is complex. The American trade paper *The Film Daily* rightly remarks that she 'gives a superbly dimensional etching of the evil mistress, suggesting much more about the character that is not touched upon in the script'.[30] *La Cinématographie française* agrees with this sentiment, arguing that, although she is harsh and calculating, nonetheless she remains very much alive – and not a cliché. Moreover, she fascinates not just as Nicole but as the star Simone Signoret.[31] *Kinematograph Weekly* puts it well: 'The serene power of Simone Signoret's playing provokes emotion.'[32] She is frightening and icy in her 'methodical murderessness', as *To-day's Cinema* so aptly puts it;[33] 'implacable' and 'business-like', to quote *The Monthly Film Bulletin*.[34] But we cannot stop watching her, because she is, as *Le Monde*'s critic rightly observes, both 'fierce and untamed' and 'enigmatic and equivocal' all at once.[35]

What these epithets make clear is that there is a dissolution of the star into the persona of Nicole, or vice versa: the one inhabits the other. It becomes hard to separate them out.[36] In all these epithets it is also clear that Signoret becomes someone onto whom we can project our fantasms. Therefore, we derive tremendous pleasure in viewing her. But I would like to suggest that we do this in several stages, which is also what gives us such a thrill in our reception of her performance. However, it is clear that we cannot project the specific fantasms of methodical murderer – nor, indeed, of femme fatale – onto her until after the film is over. Not until then do we know what she is up to. As a result, her performance is revealed as a masquerade only once we are at the end of it – once the enunciating female subject has well and truly been silenced. So what can our first reading of her be, then? Cold, hard, brusque, domineering, on the one hand, and, on the other, caring, solicitous, capable of warmth. But, above all, not overtly sexy – at least, not in the heterosexual sense. Her appearance is too 'butch' for that – so maybe lesbian pleasure can be derived in viewing. But this is surely the exact opposite from the intentionality of a film noir? Whatever the case, there is no slinky femme fatale behaviour, no false seductions where Nicole/Signoret is concerned. In fact, as I argued in Chapter 4, she spends a lot of time eschewing the role of femme fatale, conceding that space to Michel. So why do we watch fascinated? What is left to entice? I would argue that, because she is not overtly one thing, she is precisely everything. By emptying out the stereotypes, there is so much more to see. Thus, I would suggest, it is this very visible ambiguity around her sexuality that excites – invites us into knowing more about female sexuality than the simple stereotype of mistress or femme fatale would ever allow. That is Signoret's true power as a star – and we marvel at how serenely she achieves this. Devilishly clever!

Notes

1   Clouzot's film made FF 219, 781, 035 on ticket sales, while Guitry's brought a return of FF 307, 330, 850 – just over FF 80,000 more than Clouzot's film – but the Paris tickets for Guitry's film were at a higher price, so this somewhat nuances the figures in terms of audience; *Le Film français*, special Autumn issue, 1955, p. 4.
2   *Le Film français*, July 1955, p. 6.
3   *Le Film français*, special Autumn issue, 1955, p.4.
4   Bazin, André, 'Le style c'est le genre', *Cahiers du cinéma* 3 (43), 1955, pp. 42–43.
5   Tallenay, Jean-Louis, 'À diable, diable et demi, à ange, ange et demi', *Cahiers du cinéma* 3 (45), 1955, pp. 20–23.
6   Bazin (1955), p. 43.
7   Ibid., p. 43.
8   Audiberti, Jacques, 'Noir avec des coups de blanc', *Cahiers du cinéma* 3 (44), 1955, pp. 38–40.
9   See the special issue of *Avant-scène du cinéma* on Clouzot's *Le Corbeau* (186, 1977). There is a very interesting chapter on the director entitled 'Henri-Georges Clouzot' (pp. 96–118; no author name supplied), which develops these ideas concerning ambiguity.
10 I am grateful to Ginette Vincendeau for suggesting this point to me.
11 *Kinematograph Weekly*, 8 December 1955, p. 18; no author name.
12 Whitely, Reg, 'This is Xasperating, why be unfair to the kids?', *The Daily Mirror*, 2 December 1955, no page.
13 Ibid.
14 Smith, R.D., 'Vulgar, nasty – and French', *Tribune*, 16 November 1956, no page.
15 Prowse, *Sight and Sound* 25 (3), 1955/1956, p. 149.
16 Houston, Penelope, review of *Les Diaboliques*, *The Monthly Film Bulletin*, January 1956, p. 2.
17 Review of *Les Diaboliques*, *Variety*, 23 February 1956, no page.
18 Review of *Les Diaboliques*, *To-day's Cinema*, 1 December 1955, p. 10, no author name.

19   Review of *Les Diaboliques*, *The Daily Film Renter*, 1 December 1955, p. 4, no author name.
20   Review of *Diabolique*, *The Film Daily*, 22 November 1955, p. 6, no author name.
21   Houston (1956), p. 2.
22   Review of *Les Diaboliques*, *L'Humanité*, 1 February 1955, p. 2, no author name.
23   Review of *Les Diaboliques*, *L'Humanité Dimanche*, 6 February 1955, p. 10, no author name.
24   *Tribune*, 16 November 1956.
25   Houston (1956), p. 2.
26   Ibid., p. 2.
27   *The Daily Film Renter*, 1 December 1955.
28   Review of *Les Diaboliques*, *La Cinématographie française*, 5 February 1955, p. 17, no author name.
29   *Kinematograph Weekly*, 8 December 1955.
30   *The Film Daily*, 22 November 1955.
31   *La Cinématographie française*, 5 February 1955.
32   *Kinematograph Weekly*, 8 December 1955.
33   *To-day's Cinema*, 1 December 1955, p. 10.
34   Houston (1956), p. 2.
35   De Baroncelli, Jean, review of *Les Diaboliques*, *Le Monde*, 29 January 1955, p. 12.
36   Signoret speaks of her own method of acting, whereby the character enters into her, inhabits her; Signoret, Simone (1978), pp. 115–117.

Conclusion: Clouzot the auteur-philosopher and auteur-monster

Clouzot's *Les Diaboliques* won the Prix Louis Delluc for the highest film achievement in originality. Certainly, in terms of suspense, he showed himself to be a master in this film. We are kept guessing till the very end. We get lost in a tiny maze of *fausses-pistes* precisely because we are none too sure what exactly it is that we are looking for. So, when Narcejac complained that Clouzot completely demolished the original text just for effect, we, the audience, should perhaps turn around and say to him: 'Thank goodness he did.' Clouzot's ambition for the film far outstripped the quality of the novel. His lean, sparse cinematic style, the way he stripped his actors down to a degree zero, forcing them almost to be as significant or as insignificant as the objects that surround them, made him something of a phenomenological auteur. And this is, surely, part of his originality. Phenomenology was, after all, in its original manifestation, the theory of illusion – something that Clouzot is intensely preoccupied with, in this film at least. Phenomenology was also, in 1950s France, a major philosophical arena of debate, along with existentialism – one exponent of which was Jean-Paul Sartre. And, since we know that Clouzot and Sartre were friends and even shared a collaborative relationship (on a film script they subsequently abandoned), there is no reason not to suspect that Clouzot would have been familiar with the realm of these philosophical discourses.

Let us briefly consider the concept of phenomenology. Immanuel Kant gave a broad sense to the term. He distinguished between objects and events as they appear in our experience from objects and events as they are in themselves (independent from the notions imposed upon them by our cognitive faculties). Later, C.S. Pierce defined this further when he stated that phenomenology was not only a descriptive study of all that is observed to be real but also of whatever is before the mind, namely perceptions of the real, illusory perceptions, imaginations or dreams. Later still, Sartre used his own interpretation of phenomenology and worked it into his novel *La Nausée* (1938). In this novel the protagonist, Roquentin, is confronted with what could be termed a crisis in perception. Objects become endowed with power; they take on a viscous, visceral quality. The overall presence and density of things fight back at his reading of the real. Given the way that objects in Clouzot's film have a seeming energy of their own, have what we have termed 'thing-power', it becomes quite helpful to think of Clouzot in this context of phenomenology. Objects confuse us. Is that really the dead or missing headmaster in the photograph? And it is precisely because Clouzot plays with perception, makes us believe that what we are seeing is real, and does so with seemingly very real objects and events, that he succeeds in cleverly disguising the intentionality of people's acts. Thus, we believe we are following one set of intentions whereas what is really going on is another series of intentional acts altogether, which we cannot, however, decipher. We cannot read them properly precisely because we feel so assured in our ability to read the real, forgetting that objects and events are just as much independent from our perceptions as they are subjected to them. To paraphrase Edmund Husserl, we have been too caught up in cause and effect and not sufficiently attentive to the essential nature of our character's mental acts – or intentions.[1]

But the phenomenological auteur was only a part of Clouzot's ontological practice. He was the master of innovation in other ways. And, in this context, mention needs to be made of his perfectionism – which ultimately, in his case, was also an authorial sign. Interestingly, Louis Jouvet said that he sensed that Clouzot was over-preoccupied as an auteur-metteur-en-scène.[2] He saw him as being in conflict with himself because, in trying to control both the text and the technology, he was constantly in a state of tension, unable to yield, to let go of one side and pay attention to the other. In our different analyses throughout this book we have endeavoured to show how this tension has worked for Clouzot – how it is a feature of his filmmaking practice. However, Jouvet's remark is insightful, for it points also to Clouzot's autocratic demeanour and reveals the side of Clouzot that is less the playful phenomenological auteur and more the monstrous one. The one who hit his actors to get his effects. The one who rode roughshod over original novels to create his own text. The one for whom stars were creatures to be controlled. But even monsters bring about change, and, because he was so ruthless in his purpose, Clouzot was also the auteur who, as we have explained, reinvented the thriller/film noir genre, made something new happen. And, for this reason alone, Clouzot remains most assuredly one of the great film directors of the 20th century.

Notes

1   For a full discussion of phenomenology, see Schmitt, Richard (1967), pp. 135–151.
2   Bocquet (1991), p. 48.

Appendix 1: Credits

Les Diaboliques 1955

Technical Team

Director: Henri-Georges Clouzot
Production company: Filmsonor (in association with Vera Films)
Producer: Henri-Georges Clouzot
Production manager: Louis de Masure
Unit manager: Georges Testard
Assistant director: Michel Romanoff

Scenario based on novel by Pierre Boileau and Thomas Narcejac *Celle qui n'était plus*
Screenplay/dialogue: Henri-Georges Clouzot and Jérôme Géronimi (with collaboration of René Masson and Frédéric Grendel)
Script supervisor: Jeanne-Witta Montrobert

Director of photography: Armand Thirard
Camera operator: Robert Juillard
Cameramen: Louis Née, Jacques Robin, Jean Lallier
Assistant operators: Jean Dicop, Daniel Diot
Special Effects: Lax
Music: Georges Van Parys
Art director: Léon Barsacq
Sound recording: William-Robert Sivel
Editor: Madeleine Gug
Studios: Franstudio, Saint-Maurice (Paris)
Laboratories: LTC Saint-Cloud

First released 29 January 1955
The film won the Prix Louis Delluc 1955

Cast: Nicole Horner: Simone Signoret; Christina Delassalle: Vera Clouzot; Michel Delassalle: Paul Meurisse; Inspector Fichet: Charles Vanel; Monsieur Drain: Pierre Larquey; Monsieur Raymond: Michel Serreault; Plantiveau: Jean Brochard; Monsieur Herboux: Noël Roquevert; Madame Herboux: Thérèse Dorny; Moinet: Yves-Marie Maurin; Soudieu: Georges Poujoly; Patard: Henri Humbert; Ritberger: Michel Dumur; De Gascuel: Jean-Pierre Bonnefous; José: Robert Acon; a pupil: Jean-Philippe Smet (Johnny Hallyday); garagist: Robert Dalban; soldier: Jean Lefèvre; morgue attendant: Jacques Hilling; Doctor Loisy: Georges Chamarat; Professor Bridoux: Jacques Varennes; hotel employee: Jean Lefèvre.

Appendix 2: Henri-Georges Clouzot filmography

As scriptwriter-adapter

1931 *Je serais seul après minuit/I'll be Alone After Midnight* (with Pierre Gilles-Veber), director: Jacques de Baroncelli
1938 *Le Révolté/A Man Revolted* (with Jean Villard-Gilles), director: Léon Mathot
1939 *Le Duel/The Duel* (with Pierre Fresnay), director: Pierre Fresnay
1939 *Le Monde tremblera/The World Will Tremble* (with Jean Villard-Gilles), director: Richard Pottier
1941 *Le Dernier des six/The Last of the Six,* director: Georges Lacombe
1942 *Les Inconnus dans la maison/Strangers in the House,* director: Henri Decoin
1955 *Si tous les gars du monde/If all the Guys in the World* (with Jean Clouzot and Jacques Rémy), director: Christian-Jaque

As director (audience figures in parenthesis where available)

1931 *La Terreur des Batignolles/Fear in the Batignolles* (short), scenario: Jacques de Baroncelli; camera: Louis Chaix; sound: Bugnon; decor: Wilke; music: D.E. Inghelbrecht; editor: Marguerite Houlé; producer: Adolphe Osso
1942 *L'Assassin habite au 21/The Murderer Lives at Number 21,* adaptation: Henri-Georges Clouzot and Stansilas Steeman (based on S. Steeman novel); dialogue: Henri-Georges Clouzot; camera: Armand Thirard; decor: Andrei Andrejew; music: Maurice Yvain; editor: Christian Gaudin; production company: Continental Films; main cast: Pierre Fresnay, Suzy Delair, Pierre Larquey, Noël Roquevert
1943 *Le Corbeau/The Raven,* scenario: Louis Chavance; adaptation and dialogue: Louis Chavance and Henri-Georges Clouzot; camera: Nicolas Hayer; sound: William-Robert Sivel; decor: Andrei Andrejew; music: Tony Aubin; editor: Maguerite Beauge; production company: Continental Films; producer: René Montis; main cast: Pierre Fresnay, Ginette Leclerc, Micheline Francey, Pierre Larquey, Noël Roquevert
1947 *Quai des Orfèvres,* scenario, adaptation and dialogue: Jean Ferry and Henri-Georges Clouzot (based on S. Steeman's novel *Légitime défense*); camera: Armand Thirard; sound: William-Robert Sivel; decor: Max Douy; music: Francis Lopez; costumes: Jacques Fath; editor: Charles Bretoneiche; production company: Majestic Films; producer: Louis Wipf; main cast: Louis Jouvet, Suzy Delair, Bernard Blier, Simone Renant, Charles Dullin, Pierre Larquey (5.5 million audience)

1949   *Manon,* scenario, adaptation and dialogue: Jean Ferry and Henri-Georges Clouzot (based on Abbé Prévost's novel *Manon Lescaut*); camera: Armand Thirard; sound: William-Robert Sivel; decor: Max Douy; music: Paul Misraki; editor: Kirsanoff; production company: Alcina; producer: Louis Wipf; main cast: Cécile Aubry, Michel Auclair, Serge Reggiani (3.4 million audience)

1949   *Le Retour de Jean/Jean's Return* (fifth sketch of *Retour à la vie/Return to life*), scenario and dialogue: Jean Ferry and Henri-Georges Clouzot; camera: Louis Page; sound: Roger Biard; decor: Max Douy; music: Paul Misraki; editor: M. Kirsanoff; production company: Films Marceau; producer: Constantin Geftman; main cast: Louis Jouvet, Noël Roquevert, Jean Brochard

1950   *Miquette et sa mère/Miquette and her Mother,* scenario and adaptation: Jean Ferry and Henri-Georges Clouzot (based on comedy of same name by Roberto de Flers and Gaston Arman de Caillavet); dialogue: Henri-Georges Clouzot; camera: Armand Thirard; sound: William-Robert Sivel; decor: Georges Wakhévitch; music: Albert Lasry; production company: Alcina, CICC, Silver Films; producer: Paul Joly; main cast: Danièle Delorme, Louis Jouvet, Bourvil, Saturnin Fabre (2.2 million audience)

1953   *Le Salaire de la peur/Wages of Fear,* scenario, adaptation and dialogue: Jérôme Géronimi and Henri-Georges Clouzot (based on novel by Georges Annaud); camera: Armand Thirard; sound: William-Robert Sivel; decor: René Renoux; music: Georges Auric; editor: Henri Rust; production company: CICC, Silver Films, Vera Films, Fono Roma; producers: Louis Wipf, Charles Broderie; main cast: Yves Montand, Charles Vanel, Vera Clouzot (6.9 million audience)

1955   *Les Diaboliques,* scenario, adaptation and dialogue: Jérôme Géronimi, Henri-Georges Clouzot, René Masson and Frédéric Grendel (based on P. Boileau and T. Narcejeac's novel *Celle qui n'était plus*); camera: Armand Thirard; sound: William-Robert Sivel; decor: Léon Barsacq; music: Georges Van Parys; editor: Madeleine Gug; production company: Filmsonor and Vera Films; producer: Louis de Masure; main cast: Simone Signoret, Vera Clouzot, Paul Meurisse, Charles Vanel, Pierre Larquey, Noël Roquevert, Thérèse Domy, Michel Serreault (3.7 million audience)

1956   *Le Mystère Picasso,* scenario: Henri-Georges Clouzot and Pablo Picasso; camera: Claude Renoir; sound: De Bretagne; music: Georges Auric; editor: Henri Colpi; production company: Filmsonor (169, 599 audience)

1957   *Les Espions,* scenario, adaptation and dialogue: Jérôme Géronimi, Henri-Georges Clouzot (based on E. Hostovsky's novel *Vertige de minuit/Midnight Vertigo*); camera: Christian Matras; sound: William-Robert Sivel; decor: René Renoux; music: Georges Auric; editor: Madeleine Gug; production company: Filmsonor; producer: Louis de Masure; main cast: Gérard Sety, Vera Clouzot, Paul Carpenter, Curd Jurgens, Peter Ustinov, Pierre Larquey, Sach Pitoëff (1.8 million audience)

1960   *La Vérité,* scenario, adaptation and dialogue: Henri-Georges Clouzot with Vera Clouzot, Jérôme Géronimi, Simone Drieu and Michèle

Perrein; camera: Armand Thirard; sound: William-Robert Sivel; decor:
Jean André; editor: Albert Jurgenson; production company: Han-
Productions, CEIAP; producer: Louis Wipf; main cast: Brigitte Bardot,
Sami Frey; Marie-José Nat, Paul Meurisse, Charles Vanel (5.7 million
audience)

1966   *La Quatrième symphonie de Schumann,* Vienna Symphony Orchestra
under conductor Herbert von Karajan; production company: Cosmotel

1966   *Le Cinquième concerto pour violon de Mozart,* Yehudi Menuhin (violin)
Vienna Symphony Orchestra under conductor Herbert von Karajan;
Production company: Cosmotel

1966   *La Cinquième symphonie de Beethoven,* Berlin Philarmonic Orchestra
under conductor Herbert von Karajan; production company: Cosmotel

1966   *La Neuvième symphonie de Dvorak,* Berlin Philarmonic Orchestra under
conductor Herbert von Karajan; Production company: Cosmotel

1967   *Le Requiem de Verdi,* Scala Orchestra Milan under conductor Herbert
von Karajan; production company: Cosmotel

1968   *La Prisonnière,* scenario and dialogue: Henri-Georges Clouzot; camera:
Andreas Winding; sound: William-Robert Sivel; decor: Jacques Saulnier;
musical adviser: Dominique Amy; editor: Noëlle Balenci; production
company: Films Corona, Vera Films; producer: C. Hauser; main cast:
Elisabeth Wiener, Laurent Terzieff, Bernard Fresson, Dany Carrel (1.3
million audience)

Appendix 3: Select bibliography

Andrew, Geoff, entry on *Diabolique* in *Time Out Film Guide*. London, Penguin, 2001, p. 276.

Aurevilley (d') Barbey, *Les Diaboliques*. Paris, Librairie Générale Française, 1999.

Barsacq, Léon, *Le Décor de Film*. Paris, Éditions Seghers, 1970.

Bertin-Maghit, Jean-Pierre, *Le Cinéma Sous l'Occupation*. Paris, Olivier Orban, 1989.

Bocquet, José-Louis (in collaboration with Alan Godin), *Henri-Georges Léon Clouzot, Cinéaste*. Sèvres, Éditions la Sirène, 1993.

Boileau, Pierre and Narcejac, Thomas, *Celle qui n'était plus*. Paris, Éditions Denoël, 1952.

Caruth, Cathy, 'Traumatic awakenings', in A. Parker and E. Kosofsky Sedgwick (eds), *Performativity and Performance*. New York and London, Routledge, 1995, pp. 89–108.

Chalais, François, *Grands Créateurs de film* (no. 2). Paris, Jacques Vautrin, 1950.

Durant, Philippe, *Simone Signoret: Une Vie*. Lausanne and Paris, Favre, 1988.

Freud, Sigmund, *The Standard Edition of the Complete Psychological Works of Sigmund Freud*, translated and edited J. Strachey, vol. 5. London, Hogarth Press, 1953.

Krutnik, Frank, *In a Lonely Street: Film Noir, Genre, Masculinity*. London and New York, Routledge, 1991.

Hamon, Hervé, Montand, Yves and Rotman, Patrick, *Tu vois je n'ai pas oublié*. Paris, Fayard, 1990.

Mayne, Judith, *Framed: Lesbians, Feminists, and Media Culture*. Minneapolis and London, University of Minnesota Press, 2000.

Nowell-Smith, Geoffrey, 'Minnelli and melodrama', in C. Gledhill (ed.), *Home is where the Heart is*. London, British Film Institute Publishing. 1987, pp. 70–74.

Pilard, Philippe, *H-G Clouzot*. Paris, Éditions Seghers. 1969.

Pizzello, Chris, 'Bringing the dark side of the character to light in *Diabolique*', *American Cinematographer* 77 (4), 1996, pp. 36–44.

Ross, Kristin, *Fast Cars, Clean Bodies: Decolonisation and the Reordering of French Culture*. Cambridge, MA and London, MIT Press, 1995.

Santos Fontenla, César, *Clouzot*. San Sebastien, International Film Festival Publication, 1975.

Schmitt, Richard, 'Phenomenology', in P. Edwards (ed.), *The Encyclopedia of Philosophy*, vol. 5–6, L–P. New York and London, Macmillan, 1967, pp. 135–151.

Signoret, Simone, *La Nostalgie n'est plus ce qu'elle était*, (2nd edn.). Paris, Éditions du Seuil, 1978.

Votolato, Gregory, 'Barsacq', in T. Prendergast and S. Prendergast (eds), *International Dictionary of Films and Filmmakers: Writers and Production Artists*, vol. 4. London and New York, St James Press, 2000, pp. 65–67.